ORANG-UT

ORANG-UTAN

by

Barbara Harrisson

SINGAPORE
OXFORD UNIVERSITY PRESS
OXFORD NEW YORK

Oxford University Press

Oxford New York Toronto
Delhi Bombay Calcutta Madras Karachi
Petaling Jaya Singapore Hong Kong Tokyo
Nairobi Dar es Salaam Cape Town
Melbourne Auckland
and associated companies in
Berlin Ibadan

Oxford is a trade mark of Oxford University Press

First published by Collins 1962
First issued as an Oxford University Press paperback 1987
Third impression 1992

ISBN 0 19 588863 4

Printed in Malaysia by Peter Chong Printers Sdn. Bhd.
Published by Oxford University Press Pte. Ltd.,
Unit 221, Ubi Avenue 4, Singapore 1440

Contents

INTRODUCTION TO THIS EDITION   ix

DEAR COUSIN! *by Tom Harrisson*   9

I   ORANGS IN THE HOUSE   27

II   ORANGS IN THE JUNGLE   51

III EDUCATING ORANGS   89

IV   ORANGS AT SEA   137

V   ORANGS IN ZOOS   163

HAS THE ORANG A FUTURE? *with Tom Harrisson*   197

APPENDIX   I Dentitions of Orangs and Man   210
APPENDIX II Weight curves of Orang babies   212
APPENDIX III Weight curves of young Orangs   213

INDEX   214

Illustrations

Nigel	*frontispiece*
Eve in her night-sack	*facing page* 36
Eve learning to walk	37
Bidai, Eve and Bob in the garden	52
Eve and Bidai	52
Eating was Bob's principal occupation	53
A dayak long-house (*K. F. Wong*)	68
An Oran skull, revered by the dayaks	68
Gaun in the jungle	69
An Orang's nest, 30 feet above ground	69
A wild Orang in a durian tree	84
A young Orang in his nest	85
Eve, aged $2\frac{1}{2}$, with Bidai	116
Frank, Nigel and Bill (*Junaidi bin Bolhassan*)	117
Nigel in a tree	132
Bill and our otter	132
Ossy at $4\frac{1}{2}$ months	133
Janie giving Ossy his milk	164
Frank climbing while at sea	165
Nigel and Frank at their handkerchief game	165
Bad zoo conditions	180
Nigel and Frank at Hamburg Zoo	180
A mother and her baby at Frankfurt Zoo (*Tierbilder Okapia*)	181
Mickey at Edinburgh Zoo (*P. Shillabeer*)	181

*The photographs were taken by the author
except where otherwise stated*

Explanatory Note

"Orang-utan" is a Malay word now used in practically every country of the world (including Japan and Russia) to describe the ape whose scientific name is *Pongo pygmaeus*.

Commonly used hyphenated, the name derives from two separate Malay words:

> *Orang*, meaning "Man,"
> *Utan*, meaning "Jungle."

The common misusage "Orang-utang," is impertinent as being derived from the Malay word for "Debtor." Even the most cynical bio-mathematics can hardly demonstrate that it is the Orangs who are on the owing side of the modern equation.

In West Borneo, however, and in particular in Sarawak (with which country this book is mainly concerned), the Dayak term "Maias" is nearly always used, including by Malays. It is often misspelt "Mias."

Introduction to this Edition

WHEN this book was written twenty-seven years ago Sarawak, now a part of Malaysia, was still a colony. The book was written in order to draw attention to one of the most secretive and spectacular of the great apes, to prevent its mindless destruction, and to muster forces for its preservation. The book tells of Sarawak, a relatively unimportant part of Borneo from an animal's point of view. But this was where I lived, and information regarding forests outside Sarawak where these animals could be found was sketchy at best. What we know now is that Orang-utans survive in greater numbers than the book's final chapter suggested. This does not make these animals' future secure. Field studies undertaken over the past two decades suggest rather that the current methods of logging tropical forests threaten the almost total destruction of areas where Orang-utans survive.

The destitute state of mother-less Orang-utan babies, and the corruptive effect their trade had internationally, was the reason for my writing in 1961, and for experimenting shortly thereafter with alternative methods of looking after them. My idea was to try and place these orphans uncaged in a forest, where they might readjust to a natural life and eventually become self-sufficient. This was put to test between 1962 and 1965 while I was still in Sarawak. In the two decades that followed, approximately 200 orphans underwent similar programmes of rehabilitation elsewhere in Borneo and in Sumatra. They were taken to forest camps where game wardens, volunteers, students and scientists lived, supported

[ix]

by government and international agencies. These camps were located near areas where wild Orang-utans occurred. They offered the rehabilitant animals a reasonable chance of surviving in their natural habitat. Two other advantages resulted: the forests, where these camps were located, were made relatively secure, and the market for captive Orang-utans was suppressed. The economic incentives which formerly motivated hunters to kill Orang-utans–and traders to smuggle their offspring abroad–were eliminated. Nowadays, Orang-utans are very rarely killed or captured. The idea of selling babies for monetary gain or of keeping them at home as pets has lost favour. Instead, people wish to see these animals in their natural environment, and the camps where ex-captive Orang-utans undergo rehabilitation have become tourist attractions and centres for conservation education.

The apparent appeal of rehabilitation projects masks the negative aspects of such projects. It is possible for visitors to see young apes playing in trees. The fact that these youngsters are more active than those normally seen in zoos, that they are unrestrained yet apparently gentle, even tame, suggests the idea of 'paradise come true'. But this is far removed from reality. Though young apes readily climb, play, build nests and feed in trees, given a chance, this does not make them self-sufficient. The most critical component of their environment, an adult wild mother who demonstrates to them the facts of Orang-utan life and who passes on her own relationships with other wild Orang-utans, is lacking.

When I started the first rehabilitation project in 1962, it was with the aim of seeing how far the juveniles which I had in my care at home could adapt to living in the forest. Bako National Park, where the project was located, had less than 15 sq km of forest, one-third of which was mangrove and scrub where Orang-utans could not survive. There was no population of wild Orang-utans present. But the park was protected, had a visitors' centre, and was easily reached by boat from Sarawak's·capital, Kuching, where supplies and services for the animals and their attendants were readily available. Other forest areas which included wild Orang-utans would have been less secure and would have been located at greater distances. To provide supplies would have been too expensive. It was decided to start at Bako and see if the idea worked, or not to start at all. The aim was to experiment with techniques. The eventual need to relocate the animals was a consideration from the start. However, the likelihood of the Orang-utans concerned becoming self-sufficient in Bako and maintaining themselves there long-term was only small.

The techniques employed were relatively simple. We erected a large wire-mesh cage in the forest where the animals could be confined initially. We gradually let them go free, while also support-feeding them and taking them into the reserve as far as they would follow us. Though this seemed successful initially, problems remained which proved difficult to overcome.

These problems largely had to do with the role we, as humans, had to assume under these circumstances. However vivacious our animals were when unconfined, it was clear from the start that their urge to explore the forest independently was limited. As soon as the animals were left to themselves, they went in search of human companionship. They drifted in the direction of the beach where their attendants had their camp and from whence they appeared at intervals. However, at Bako, this beach was also frequented by tourists. The fear of bathers when suddenly confronted with an Orang-utan is easy to imagine. Fortunately, Orang-utans cannot swim and one can easily avoid them by going into the water. But most people do not know this and can hurt themselves by getting entangled with an animal whose physical strength they cannot match.

The cage we had built was of hardwood poles covered with chain-link wire. It enclosed small trees and was itself surrounded by trees. The initial confinement of the animals lasted only three days. Then the door was opened. Food platforms were erected in the forest and food was offered there. When evening fell, the attendants left the animals near the cage. The larger animal, Arthur, built nests for himself overlooking it, where he spent the night. The smaller animals, Cynthia and George, went inside the cage to sleep on platforms which we had built.

The single most characteristic behaviour of young Orangutans is to quietly observe and then manipulate or test the object of their interest. Even though for our animals their new environment was as varied as any forest could be, the target of their interest remained human–the individuals who cared for them daily, and, by extension, anyone who visited. After a few months, we had to admit one mistake. We had built the cage too close to areas where park visitors could be expected. Arthur was already four years old and his way of testing human strength could not be trusted.

We abandoned the first cage and built a new one in a part of the park where visitors did not normally go. Here the animals were able to remain for two years, support-fed and attended by men who were based at a camp in the vicinity. Arthur was partial to perching in high trees from which he had a view of the beach and of the supply-boats arriving. Whenever he heard the noise of an outboard-motor, he would go down to investigate. By the time a boatman had his craft in the shallows, he was waiting on the beach.

As a six-year old Arthur was adolescent, frequently rough, unpredictable and sometimes difficult to handle. He might have been left to survive on his own, but he remained attracted to humans. We knew we would have to transfer him to some other area. Bako Park could not be closed to visitors. It had to remain open, and the public's safety there had to be guaranteed.

Both Arthur and Cynthia originally came from Sabah, 2 000 km up the coast. Sabah's game authorities were prepared to take them both back, and to make the animals part of Sabah's own rehabilitation project which was then being started. The project was located in the vicinity of Sandakan, Sabah's major port on the east coast, on the edge of a protected forest named Sepilok, which included wild Orangutans.

During the days and nights when the launch which carried our animals steamed eastward, Arthur steadily worked at taking his cage to pieces. We repaired it as fast as he succeeded in destroying it, and as best as was possible in the circumstances. We finally unloaded him at Sandakan, re-loaded him on to a lorry and then carried him, in his cage, to the edge of Sepilok's forest. Here the cage broke. Alarmed and frustrated by his long confinement, Arthur dashed up the nearest tree. Our hope was that he would remain at a distance.

Repeatedly we coaxed him deep into the forest, leaving him at fair distances from the camp at nightfall. But he remained attracted to the camp, where men lived, where food was stored, and where other Orang-utans were to be found. Inevitably he came into camp one day when the men who knew him well were away. He raided the camp, where frightened men were unable to stop him or chase him away. Finally one, who believed himself cornered when he came on the scene, got his gun. He shot Arthur dead, believing he was acting in self-defence.

Sepilok was not far from Sandakan. The base camp, at the end of a motor-road, was serviced by veterinary officers and suppliers. Forest stretched in three directions. Cages had been built for the care of confiscated wild animals and birds which people had caught or held unlicenced. Young Orangutans among them were not just the victims of poachers who had intended to sell them. They were also the victims of loggers who worked in forests where wild Orang-utans occurred.

The animals were looked after in the same way as at Bako. New arrivals were put in quarantine for a month or more. Depending on their age and state of health, they were released into trees while being support-fed in the forest. Cages remained temporary abodes for animals not yet ready to remain free. Quickly Sepilok became a tourist attraction. The camp's most famous Orang-utan was Joan, an adult female, who, after years of captivity, went free, mated with a wild male and, to everyone's delight, returned to the camp just before giving birth to a fine baby. Although she was able to nurse her baby, she accepted extra food during the first weeks of her motherhood and remained close to the camp for a long time. Cynthia, Arthur's old companion, was less enterprising than Joan. Even when she was nearly adult, she preferred to stay in the camp. She liked the company of Orang-utans smaller than herself and in Sepilok, there was no shortage of them. During the early 1970s, most new arrivals came from timber camps.

When Stanley de Silva, Sabah's game warden, became known internationally for his work in Sepilok, questions regarding the Orang-utans of Sumatra and their chances of survival were raised. Physically, the Sumatran Orang-utans are very much like those of Borneo. Adult males grow a little larger, and all Sumatran animals appear lighter in hair colour. The Leuser Reserve in the north of Sumatra, where they occurred, included vast stretches of protected forest, but only portions of it was inhabited by Orang-utans, and these appeared to be on the reserve's fringes, where squatters and settlers were pressing for new land, slowly getting a greater hold of more and more forest for cultivation.

Convinced that the Leuser Reserve and its Orang-utan population required special support, the Netherlands Appeal of the World Wildlife Fund collected money in Holland. A field station was built at Ketambe in the Allas valley, at a point where the fast-flowing Allas delimited and protected the fringes of the Leuser Reserve. Crossing the river was difficult. A short distance away, in a clearing, a camp was built together with a caged enclosure for captives. The intention was to use Ketambe for the rehabilitation of captive Orang-utans and simultaneously as a base from which to conduct systematic observations of wild Orang-utans. Herman Rijksen, a Dutch zoologist, went to work there. Together with his wife Ans, he took care of captive Orang-utans which the authorities had confiscated. Getting hold of them was difficult at first. Though it was against the law to keep Orang-utans, the people of that area regarded it as a normal practice and, up to that point, the government had done nothing to stop it.

The Rijksens, who looked after rehabilitants in Ketambe between 1971 and 1973, while also getting acquainted with the wild Orang-utans of their vicinity, became convinced that it was better to separate rehabilitation from their other work of observation. The physical aspects of Ketambe were ideal for the study of wild Orang-utans. The area also seemed to contain more individuals per square kilometre of forest than had been observed elsewhere. For rehabilitation, on the other hand, Ketambe was rather too isolated. Resident tigers endangered the smaller animals, and because wild Orang-utans frequented the forest right down to the camp, the risk of disease being passed via the rehabilitant animals or the people who cared for them to the wild population, had to be considered. Another consideration was that released rehabilitants might cause stress to the wild population by increasing the number of Orang-utans beyond the capacity of the Ketambe area.

At this time, large numbers of captives still existed in the vicinity of Medan, and new efforts had to be made to get hold of them. Bohorok, a new rehabilitation centre, was thus built in the Langkat Reserve, a few hours' drive from Medan. It was first funded by the Frankfurt Zoological Society. The major goal of those who worked there, the Swiss zoologists Regine Frey and Monika Boerner, and the English zoologists Conrad and Rosalind Aveling, was to take in as many captives as they could get hold of, rehabilitate and release them, and to provide grassroots conservation education among the local community. Owners of captive Orang-utans had to be con-

[xv]

vinced that giving their animals up was the right thing to do. They were encouraged to visit the station and to bring others along.

Between 1973 and 1979, no fewer than 98 captive Orang-utans were taken to Bohorok. Well over half of them had been held captive in the homes of government officials, and plant-ation-, timber-, or oil-concessioneers. The rest were from dealers or villagers previously linked with the lucrative export market of babies. Thousands of visitors came to Bohorok, 80 per cent of them Indonesian. Fifty people at a time were allowed to cross the Bohorok River, the natural barrier which separated the animals and the centre from the unprotected world.

The methods employed at Bohorok resembled those of other projects. New arrivals were kept in quarantine, where veterinary checks were made and vaccinations and other treatment were given. Release in the forest followed, while support food was given. In Bohorok, uninteresting food was deliberately given in order to encourage the animals to forage on their own. The sites where food was left were changed frequently, so as to forestall the destruction of vegetation and prevent debris from building up. As soon as the animals were observed building nests in trees for the night, they were left in the forest overnight. Other animals were placed into cages overnight, where they were looked after alongside babies.

The final stage of rehabilitation was for the animals to drift off and stay away, or, alternatively, to be taken by helicopter about 20 km away for release. This was possible for animals aged four or older, and when an animal was in an appropriate condition. Bohorok's adult females rehabilitated more easily than others, evidently because of associations they formed with wild males. Juvenile and adolescent males found it difficult by comparison. They retreated from wild males, or, if they failed to do so, got bitten by them. Of twenty-five animals released by helicopter during the 1970s, only two were observed months after release in a healthy condition. Of others one can be less sure. Though they were followed for a few days, the steep valleys and ridges of the forest made follow-up very difficult. To remain close to a released animal for any length of time was also undesirable. Continuing contact could only hamper its chances of getting in touch with wild Orang-utans.

Less in the tourist limelight than either Bohorok or Sepilok was Tanjong Puting in Indonesian Borneo, where Birute Galdikas had gone to live. When I visited her during the first year of her research in 1971, she shared a small hut with her husband Rod, two rehabilitant Orang-utans plus the occasional human visitor. I was her first visitor. I remember squeezing in between doorpost and Orang-utan limbs. Rather than build a facility for her 'captive' Orang-utans, Birute integrated them into her modest home. She was unmoved by the fact that they took it to pieces, raided her supplies, draped themselves with her shirts and, mostly, around her. Her life's dream was to study Orang-utans. She wanted little besides. At Tanjong Puting, there was no tourist traffic, no running water, electricity or drainage. Her house was built with hammer and saw.

Adult Orang-utans are solitary. Males wander through the forest looking for the fruits which constitute their diet. Females, usually in the company of one or two of their offspring, do likewise. To get these animals accustomed to an observing human, and for that human to understand how these animals manage to survive individually and socially as a species, requires persistence, patience and devotion over years. Birute had all these qualities and managed to get support for her work as well. The Leakey Foundation and the National Geographical Society of America, the World Wildlife Fund and the Indonesian government combined to sponsor her work in various ways. Now in her eighteenth year of study at Tanjong Puting, the vast game reserve is destined to become a national park. Her camp, a cluster of permanent buildings, with facilities and employment for about seventy guards, workers, students and visitors, has become a valuable asset for the entire region, which is otherwise devoid of development being of little use to agriculture and having no known mineral wealth.

The captive Orang-utans which Birute took in during the 1970s had similar backgrounds to those of Sepilok or Bohorok. Convinced that they could add to her understanding of wild Orang-utans and assist in forming relationships with wild individuals, she took them piggyback with her into the forest, where she remained quietly under trees occupied by wild Orang-utans. A decade of persistent observation taught her that immature Orang-utans, be they adolescent females or sub-adult males, can be more sociable than their elders, and that sexual maturity changes that. Males become aggressive, often deadly dangerous at this point, while females become impregnated, solitary and devoted to their offspring, whom they permit to remain close until aged four of five. Then the female's powerful jaws and canines teach the offspring to get away, and get on with life alone.

The surrogate mother that I had once been, and that Birute and others continue to be for young Orang-utans, cannot teach this important lesson. Among the most agonizing of my experiences was when Arthur was killed. Birute had a similar experience when she realized that the first male she had brought up from infancy–one who had curled around me in sleep aged one–acted out his jealousy at the age of seven by killing a younger animal who was then being mothered by Birute. The jealousy of adult males can indeed be deadly. Birute herself had a narrow escape from death when she took an ex-captive female, who was already adult, piggyback from the forest to her camp. Luckily the wild male who had become interested in this female and had pursued her, did not attack Birute, only glared at her. He later became father to that female's first baby much to everyone's astonishment. The female had been held captive in a small cage for over six years and when it first arrived in 1975, it could not walk or even open its hands. At first the animal refused food, but after a few months it began to regain the use of its limbs. Finally in 1977, it gave birth to a baby.

Orang-utans are the largest-bodied fruit-eaters on earth. Long-term observation has revealed that they consume more than 300 types of fruit, bark, and flowers, as well as occasional insects and honey. Though they are solitary, they maintain complex habits and relationships which take advantage of the peculiar conditions of their forest home. The home range of an adult Orang-utan is rarely more than 6 sq km, the daily range less than 1 sq km. The greatest previous threat to Orang-utans was hunting pressure and the illegal trade in juveniles. Owing to the impact of the rehabilitation projects, this pressure has been lifted. In terms of profit, killing Orang-utans in order to obtain a captive baby has become pointless. While local governments now confiscate every animal which happens to have an accident and keep it in official care, the forests, where rehabilitation projects are located, are secure, while the residents in the vicinity of the projects have become interested in conservation and the study of nature. The projects which continue into the 1980s thereby counteract current economic strategies which destroy the forest. Though Orang-utans range much more widely than previously assumed, it has become clear that the forests upon which their future depends are being eliminated.

The majority of Orang-utans survive in Indonesia, approximately 30,000 of them in central and southern Borneo and another 5,000 in northern Sumatra. However, only populations living in parks and reserves have a reasonable chance of survival, and only the largest parks can harbour viable wild populations. The great hope of the future is Indonesia's own conservation movement, its gaining political effectiveness and strength. International agencies, such as the World Wildlife Fund or the Food and Agricultural Organization of the United Nations, will continue to support countries whose territories include tropical forests. But

INTRODUCTION

essentially it is up to Indonesia and Malaysia to resist commercial logging of the forest in reserves, to ensure that new reserves are created for threatened animals and plants, and to see that they become exempt from resettlement programmes.

The success of the rehabilitation programmes and the capacity of Orang-utans to breed in zoos may suggest to some that these animals have a future under conditions of semi-captivity. This is not so. Only a wild population of reasonable size can maintain itself and pass on the behaviour and experiences it takes to survive in the tropical forest.

Leeuwarden, The Netherlands   BARBARA HARRISSON
April 1987

DEAR COUSIN!

Tom Harrisson

While his external form will probably ever remain unchanged, except in the development of that perfect beauty which results from a healthy and well-organised body, refined and ennobled by the highest intellectual faculties and sympathetic emotions, his mental constitution may continue to advance and improve till the world is again inhabited by a single homogeneous race, no individual of which will be inferior to the noblest specimens of existing humanity.

Alfred Russel Wallace;
in Borneo, 1854-6

THE ORAN = OOTAN

From Beeckman's *A Voyage to and from the Island of Borneo*, 1714

To-day Orangs are confined to small sectors of Sumatra and Borneo. Even within these two islands, they were much commoner and more widespread in the recent past.

When man, in his early forms as *Pithecanthropus* of Java and *Gigantopithecus* of China, first began to thrive in far Asia, Orang-utans were plentiful and widespread through all this part of the world. Remains have been found in Stone Age archæological sites from Peking to the Celebes. Dubois, the discoverer of *Pithecanthropus*, found great numbers of non-fossil Orang teeth in limestone caves around the Padang Highlands of central Sumatra. In the last five years, similar non-fossil Orang teeth have been found in the Sarawak Museum's excavations at the Niah Caves and elsewhere in West Borneo, up to 200 miles from the nearest Orang living to-day. In the Great Caves of Niah, we have excavated cooked Orang bone at least to the level of 35,000 B.C. in the early Stone Age or Palaeolithic. The earlier of these Orang remains tend to be longer in the tooth than any known in historic times— indicating a gradual decline in overall size in the past dozen or so millennia.

At Niah, there is a high preponderance of female and young, as represented by sexually identifiable teeth and bones. From other evidence we already think that the Stone Age cave-men of Niah had few devices for catching large arboreal animals. They evidently best tackled Orangs by isolating a mother with baby, in much the same way as later-day zoo collectors have regularly done, with devastating effect.

There are also indications from the cave earth of Niah that far back in the Stone Age Orangs may have been kept as pets by the cave-men.[1] It is clear, then, that Asians were intimate with

[1] On prehistoric Orang remains in Borneo see Dr. D. A. Hooijer, Prof. G. H. R. V. Koenigswald and Lord Medway, reports in the

the Orang thousands of years ago ; and it is probable that long before this ape was known to western science, men were killing or keeping it in semi-captivity.

But early men seldom—in tropical Asia anyway—spoiled a good thing through excess. The bread of jungle living is thickly buttered on the side of *controlled* hunting and mild conservation.

Although the first clear proof of the Orang's existence in western records comes less than 400 years ago, it is a curious and faintly ironical fact—recently demonstrated by Dr. Kenneth Oakley of the British Museum—that the lower jaw of the Pilt-down Man forgery is probably slightly older than this. Partly as a result of evidence we were able to provide from Sarawak, Dr. Oakley and the late Professor de Vries have suggested[1] that this jaw, which the forger Dawson doctored and for nearly half a century passed off as "human," was that of an Orang obtained from Chinese gold washings in a Sarawak cave.

Be that as it may, in 1641 a Dutchman, Nicholas Tulp, was apparently the first to use the name "Orang-utan" in a scientific context, though this was applied by him to a Chimpanzee from Angola. By this time, probably, the Malay Archipelago stories of the Orang were already current—the first European having reached Borneo more than a century before. Shortly afterwards, another Dutchman, Jacob Bontius, a doctor in Java, correctly applied the name to the Sumatran and Bornean animal.

Dr. Bontius, whose descriptions were subsequently incor-porated in Buffon's great *Natural History*, saw "with admiration" some individuals of this species "walking erect on two feet" and he gives a drawing of

"a female who seemed to have an idea of modesty, covering herself with her hand on the appearance of men with whom she

Sarawak Museum Journal, Vol. VIII nos. 12-16, 1959-61, which also publishes papers on live Orang and other studies in detail. (Available from Curator, Sarawak Museum, Kuching, Sarawak.)

[1] *Nature*, 184, 1959 : 224.

12

was not acquainted; who sighed, cried, and did a number of other actions, so like the human race, that she wanted nothing of humanity but the gift of speech."

Sometimes, here and hereafter, one uneasily feels that in those early days, sharp Malays passed off cretinous step-sisters on credulous scientists, in this thirst for sensation and data.

Bontius also reported local opinion, which proved (naturally) to be characteristically conditioned by one side of Indonesian ideology:

"The Javanese maintain that these animals can speak but refuse to do so for fear of being made to work."[1]

The first Englishman enters the Orang scene with honest Edward Tyson: Oxford Don; London physician; Fellow of the Royal Society. He managed to get hold of an infant Chimpanzee which had died on the journey from Angola to London. His report was dedicated to Lord John Summers, under the title: *Orang-Outang : Or the Anatomy of a Pygmy Compared with That of a Monkey, an Ape and a Man* (1698).

The first Englishman to *visit* actual Orang territory and leave a description thereof was Captain Daniel Beeckman, who came to south (Dutch) Borneo in 1712. In his *A Voyage to and from the Island of Borneo* (1714) this tough merchant sailor wrote:

"The Monkeys, Apes, and Baboons are of many different Sorts and Shapes; but the most remarkable are those they call Oran-ootans, which in their Language signifies Men of the Woods: these grow up to be six Foot high; they walk upright, have longer Arms than Men, tolerable good Faces (handsomer I am sure than some *Hottentots* that I have seen), large Teeth, no Tails nor Hair, but on those Parts where it grows on humane Bodies; they are very nimble footed and mighty strong; they throw great Stones, Sticks, and Billets at those Persons that offend them. The Natives do really

[1] See on this: S. Heuvelmans *On the Track of Unknown Animals*, London, 1958, p. 110.

believe that these were formerly Men, but Meta-morphosed into Beasts for their Blasphemy."

Beeckman also had the doubtful honour of being the first Briton and one of the first westerners to purchase a live Orang (or cretin) on the spot—for the equivalent of about £1 (sterling).

"I bought one out of curiosity, for six *Spanish* Dollars ; it lived with me seven Months, but then died of a Flux ; he was too young to show me many Pranks, therefore I shall only tell you that he was a great Thief, and loved strong Liquors ; for if our Backs were turned, he would be at the Punch-bowl, and very often would open the Brandy Case, take out a Bottle, drink plentifully, and put it very carefully into its place again. He slept lying along in a human Posture with one Hand under his Head. He could not swim, but I know not whether he might not be capable of being taught."

The French naturalist Buffon (1707-1788) drew heavily on Tyson and Bontius, but was one of many who now proceeded further to confuse the Orang proper and the Chimpanzee.[1] In the end this got sorted out, and the scientific name *Pongo pygmaeus* given to the Orang, after a considerable period when the Chimpanzee was also referred to as *Pongo*. Buffon (*A Natural History, General and Particular*, translation by W. Smelley, London, 1791, Vol. VIII) wrote :

". . . This Orang-outang or pongo is only a brute, but a brute of a kind so singular, that man cannot behold it without contemplating himself, and without being thoroughly convinced that his body is not the most essential part of his nature."

The great Swedish naturalist Linnaeus (1707-1778) was in

[1] Not that this sort of confusion is confined to the earlier centuries. During the latter part of 1960 we spent considerable time completing three "Borneo Jungle" films for Granada TV in England. One of these was about Orangs. A producer referred in written memoranda and in detail to what he thought we should do in presenting to the educated type of viewer our "Borneo Chimpanzees."

similar trouble. In the 10th edition of his *System of Nature* (1758) he puts with *Homo sapiens* another creature called *"Homo nocturnus"* or *"Homo sylvestris orang-outang."* Of it he wrote :

> "It lives within the boundaries of Ethiopia (Pliny), in the caves of Java, Amboina, Ternate. Body white, walks erect, less than half our size. Hair white, frizzled. Eyes orbicular ; iris and pupils golden. Vision lateral, nocturnal. Life-span twenty-five years. By day hides; by night it sees, goes out, forages. Speaks in a hiss. Thinks, believes that the earth was made for it, and that sometime it will be master again, if we may believe the travellers."

This supposed Orang ambition has fortunately not since been noticed by anxious mankind. Not that any additional excuses have been necessary, since 1758, to incite people to treat Orangs as somehow basely inimical to human mastery.

By the later half of the eighteenth century a number of Orangs had been brought to Europe, mostly from Dutch-controlled Sumatra to Holland. The director of the Prince of Orange's private zoo obtained a live female from Borneo in 1776 and kept it at home for a month under observation, until the pressure of "public curiosity forced him to place it in the menagerie."[1]

The Prince of Orange's Orang did not survive long, of course, and was sent to another Dutch scientist, Petrus Camper, for dissection. Camper (1722-1789) was the first man to go in for Orangs in a big way, dead—although before long the scale of his operations was to pale into insignificance by comparison with Alfred Russel Wallace and other evolutionists of the following century. By now, the erroneous and complicating belief had developed that there were at least two different races of

[1] On this and much else in the early scientific history of anthropoidology, see the study by Prof. John C. Greene, *The Death of Adam*. Iowa State University Press, 1959, an excellent work.

Orang, probably several (a misconception still surviving without adequate justification).

Between 1778 and 1782 Camper published extensively on the Orang, with particular reference to its capacity (or otherwise) for speech. We hear here a faint echo of the horrible experiment undertaken five centuries earlier in Germany when Frederick II gave orders to bring up a number of new-born children "without ever talking to or joking with them"—in order to find out about original speech. The experiment failed, however, because "they were unable to live without the loving chatter of their nurses."

From the nineteenth century onwards there are literally hundreds of scientific papers on Orangs, dealing with every minute aspect of their physique—and often going on to make deductions about the attributes supposed to follow from physical characteristics described.[1] It does not appear to have occurred to anybody to go (or send a student) and study what Orangs actually did in the wild. No serious attempt has been made to observe Orangs under natural conditions ; my wife's is a small beginning.

The satisfaction of murdering such near-humans without penalty of law—they being unable to answer back—continued to prove attractive. The new ideas triggered off by Darwin and Wallace, placing ever greater emphasis on apes, only added fresh incentive.

Now they become better than brutes but very directly reflections on the human race as well : disreputable and often unwanted, unless (like Chimpanzees) they could be taught to *ape* the man.

Alfred Russel Wallace, co-founder of evolutionary theory in

[1] The Museum of Natural History in Paris acquired, probably in 1796 and from Holland, a first skeleton of an adult Orang. But this was thought to be a Giant Baboon until 1829. Much of the credit for sorting out the early disorder in the skeletal taxonomy of the great apes is due to Richard Owen. He published an excellent series of drawings comparing juvenile and adult Orang and Chimpanzee, in the *Transactions of the Zoological Society of London* for 1835. Nothing so good on Orangs has been published there since.

the popular sense, and a definitive figure in the evolution of all modern thought, was attracted to come to Borneo, partly because of the Orang-utan. His greatest work, *The Malay Archipelago* (1893) is sub-titled for the Orang (of Borneo) and the Bird of Paradise (of New Guinea), which are respectively used to illustrate the title pages of the first edition's two volumes.

Wallace selected Sarawak in Borneo for his first and most intensive field study in the East, partly because of the encouragement of the White Rajah of Sarawak (Sir James Brooke), partly because of the abundance there of the Orang, already the focus of so much laboratory and captivity interest in the West. Writing home from Lingga River in May, 1855, he said :

> "One of the principal reasons which induced me to come here, was that it is the country of those most strange and interesting animals, the orang-utangs, or "mias" of the Dayaks . . ."

In those days, however, the words "ecology," "ethology" and such-like, had not been invented. Natural history was not necessarily done by observation, but equally (and more easily) by assassination. Thus in the same letter Wallace goes on :

> "I have already been fortunate to shoot two young animals of two of the species, which were easily distinguishable from each other, and I hope by staying here to get adult specimens of all species, and also to obtain much valuable information as to their habits."

The hope of further "specimens" was amply justified in the event. In the following month, for instance :

> "On June 4th, some Dayaks came to tell us that the day before a Mias had nearly killed one of their companions. A few miles down the river there is a Dayak house, and the inhabitants saw a large Orang feeding on the young shoots of a palm by the river-side. On being alarmed he *retreated* towards the jungle which was close by, and a number of men armed with spears and choppers, ran out to intercept him.

The man who was in front tried to run his spear through the animal's body, but the Mias seized it in his hands, and in an instant got hold of the man's arm, which he seized in his mouth, making his teeth meet in the flesh above the elbow, which he tore and lacerated in a dreadful manner. Had not the others been close behind, the man would have been more seriously injured, if not killed, as he was quite powerless ; but they soon *destroyed* the creature with their spears and choppers. . . They told me the dead Mias was still lying where it had been killed, so I offered them a reward to bring it up to our landing-place immediately, which they promised to do."

This sort of conduct on the part of apes, interfering with man— and worse still, woman—only made a pleasant scientific task righteously delightful. Thus a fortnight later, we find the great naturalist—who was also a great humanitarian, vegetarian, conservationist, radical socialist, money reformer and spiritualist— writing like this :

"On June 18th I had another *great* success, and obtained a fine adult male. A Chinaman told me he had seen him feeding by the side of the path to the river, and I found him at the same place as the first individual I had shot. He was feeding on an oval green fruit having a fine red arillus, like the mace which surrounds the nutmeg, and which alone he seemed to eat, biting off the thick outer rind and dropping it in a continual shower. I had found the same fruit in the stomach of some others which I had killed. Two shots caused this animal to loose his hold, but he hung for a considerable time by one hand, and then fell flat on his face and was half-buried in the swamp. For several minutes he lay groaning and panting, while we stood close round, expecting every breath to be his last. Suddenly, however, by a violent effort he raised himself up, causing us all to step back a yard or two, when, standing nearly erect, he caught hold of a small tree, and began to ascend it. Another shot through the back caused him to fall down dead. A flattened bullet was found in his tongue, having entered the lower part of the abdomen and completely traversed the body, fracturing the first cervical vertebra. Yet it was after this fearful wound that he had risen, and begun climbing with considerable facility. This also was a full-grown male of almost exactly the same dimension as the other two I had measured. . . . On June 21st I shot another adult female, which was eating fruit in a low tree, and was the only one *which I ever killed by a single ball.*"

More than fifty years after he had left Borneo, Wallace, now a kindly old vegeterian looked back to those Orang days in his *Studies Scientific and Social* (London, 1912) without anger:

"While shooting these animals in Borneo for their skins and skeletons, I often saw them pass from tree to tree in this way, and they generally were able to travel through the forest overhead as quickly as I could run along underneath, looking up frequently to keep them in sight. Once I saw one build a nest. I had wounded him severely and expected he would drop to the ground, but he got up as high as he could into the tree ; choosing a forked branch he stretched out his arms, broke off or cracked the smaller branches and laid them across the fork, and in a short time had made a platform which completely hid him from below. The next day he was still there but dead, as could be seen from the cloud of flies above him. He was a very fine large male and I obtained the bones sometime afterwards by paying a dollar to two Malays who climbed the tree, and tying the dried skin with a long cord, let it down to the ground."

Wallace was "fortunate" enough to sail into a receptive Bornean atmosphere. The White Rajah of Sarawak and his friends had already interested themselves in Orangs and initiated a general slaughter of them—for although the Dutch had penetrated the Orang areas of Sumatra and south and east Borneo long before, no European had yet entered the similar sectors of north and west Borneo (in what are still the "British" parts of the island) until well on in the nineteenth century.

A little before Wallace came to Sarawak, Captain Rodney Mundy, R.N., highly esteemed editor of Sir James Brooke's early journals (*Narrative of Events in Borneo and Celebes*, 1848, Vol. I) indulged himself characteristically at the Orangs' expense:

> "Whilst employed in taking these bearings, word was brought of more orang outangs, so off I set forgetting geography in the ardour of sport. It was—*to my disappointment*—another female with her young. The young one was shot in the arms of the parent, which when severely wounded let it go, then twisting the boughs into a nest quietly seated herself, and in a short time expired without falling, and causing us considerable trouble to get her down, for the tree was lofty and difficult to climb."

The sporting captain adds further fresh comment:

> "Rajak Ali (the Datu Jembrang's son) enjoyed the sport keenly and assured me he would catch any *mias*, even of the largest size, with a few men. The way, as he explained it, was as follows:—Having discovered the animal in a tree, they approach without disturbing him, and as quietly as possible cut down all the trees round the one he is in. Being previously provided with poles, some with nooses attached to the ends and others forked, they fell the isolated tree, and the *mias* confused, entangled, is beset by his pursuers, noosed, forked down and made captive. I doubt not this mode may be adopted with success when the trees are not thick, and, at any rate, I have made Rajak Ali promise to try to procure me a large *mias pappan* by offering him thirty dollars (£4) for one as tall as a man."

Some years later, Mr. Frederick Boyle, F.R.G.S. (*Adventures among the Dyaks of Borneo*, 1865, p. 275), reports:

> "The great abundance of fruit at Banting naturally attracts

thither numbers of the various birds and animals which live upon such food. In especial the spot is haunted by the 'mias,' and, in fact, this is the only locality at present known where they can always be procured. The gentleman who we found assisting Mr. Chambers in his mission labours had, in the course of a few months, shot eight of these animals, which are destructive, though *in no way dangerous*."

Needless to say there have been no Orangs anywhere near the Anglican Mission at Banting (Lingga River) within living memory. But when a single, unnamed, unrecorded padre could shoot eight in a few months (presumably to protect the first fruit of his baptised flock ?), the amazing thing is that any Orangs survived anywhere. Of course, neither men of God nor men of science would have dared such indiscriminate assault if it had not been sanctioned by Higher Authority.

We know, for instance, that the royal Brookes kept pets. Another naval man, Midshipman Frank Marryat (*Borneo and the Indian Archipelago*, 1848, p. 103) has left one of these on the record :

"After passing two very pleasant days at Kuchin, we pre-pared to descend the river. I have omitted to say that Mr. Treecher, the surgeon, was fond of natural history, and possessed a very tolerable collection of birds, and other animals indigenous to the country. I was shown several skeletons of the Orang outang, some of which were of great size. There is no want of these animals in the jungle, but a living specimen is not easy to procure ; I saw but one, an adult female, belonging to Mr. Brooke. It was very gentle in its manners, and, when standing upright, might have measured three feet six inches."

A third and very famous sailor, Captain Henry Keppel, later Admiral of the Fleet, an intimate friend and ally of James Brooke, also went in for Orangs in quite a big way. At one stage, after boasting (*The Expedition to Borneo of H.M.S. Dido*, 1846, Vol. 1, pp. 76-77) about

"the immense size of the *hand* in my possession"

and his other Orang materials (including a live baby " received from the Rajah") he declares he will pursue knowledge more vigorously in order to settle uncertainties about the different kinds of this great ape :

"the facts are wanting, and these facts I doubt not I can soon procure . . ."

Such enthusiastic amateur procurement was yearly stuff in the British part of Borneo for nearly three-quarters of a century. But by the beginning of the present one, so great a toll had been taken that Orangs were no longer readily available for the Anglican priest with a shotgun and Monday off or the naval officer with short shore leave and the longing to kill on land.

Perhaps the last "civilised man" to get the full benefit of easy apeicide was the famed American collector, William Hornaday, who afterwards increased the ratio of remorse in his bloodstream —as quite a few ageing hunters do—and helped found the New York Zoo. His *Two Years in the Jungle* (1885) is the last clear description of free-for-all Orang swatting. In 1878 this one man alone accounted for at least forty Orangs removed, dead, dying or alive, from Sarawak.

By the turn of the century, when the great botanist, Count Beccari, visited Borneo (*Wanderings in the Forests of the Far East*, 1906) the ethics of gentlemanhood were changing somewhat. The credit to be got by presenting an Orang skull to your old school or medical college had by now been diminished—by saturation. Orangs were also becoming scarcer and harder to find. At the same time, the wish to see wild animals alive was growing ; soon the zoo demand for Orangs becoming acute. The Dutch in Sumatra and East Borneo, the Brookes in Sarawak, began to show a little more humane interest in wild life ; though no conservation law was passed in the latter country until after the

Brookes ceded the territory to Britain, in 1946. In North Borneo, which was then run by a very business-like chartered company, even vague psychological horror of Orang slaughter was slower to show. As late as 1913 we have an account (*British North Borneo* by L. W. W. Gudgeon; Chapter x, "The Orang-utan"):

> "When the child or woman who is on the watch shouts out that a '*kogyu*,' which is the local name of the ape in the hill villages, is in the fruit-trees, then half a dozen men and boys seize their 'sumpitans' [blow-pipes] and creeping round the base of the tree, they fire volley after volley of small inch-long darts at the red hairy body of the ape. If he is on a low branch, he is soon overcome by the poison and falls. But if high up, it is probable that the one or two darts that reach him only sting him into a fury. He dashes to and fro, shaking the branches of the tree as violently as ever they were shaken by a gale. The fruit falls in all directions. If it is 'durian' or 'tarap,' the size and weight of which are considerable, the Dusuns stand clear, for even a Dusun skull is not proof against such a bombardment.
>
> "The Dusuns credit the 'orang-utan' with devilish malignity, but as a matter of fact the poor creature is a great deal more frightened of them than they are of him. The Dusuns often capture young ones, and tie them up with a piece of rattan-cane, on which they have threaded joints of hard bamboo to prevent their biting through it. These youngsters soon become tame."

Mr. Gudgeon ends his chapter smugly enough :

> "When kept as domestic pets by Europeans they become very affectionate, and, unless teased, can be trusted in every way. Of course, they cannot be let loose. . . ."

I wish Mr. Gudgeon had been right. My home-life might have been a *lot* easier these last few years.

Broadly, then, in the first half of the twentieth century there was less crude slaughter of Orangs and other apes under the pretext of natural science, Christian sport, or the protection of indigenous rights. But the poor apes were now increasingly caged for human delight. In order to cage one, invariably *at least* one other had to be killed—unless special methods (not at first known or generally practicable) were employed. Those taken captive frequently died before they reached their intended zoos. Of the survivors, less than one in five survived more than three years' captivity, though an Orang's normal expectation of life is at least twenty-five years.

The mortality rate is much the same to-day; so, beneath the veneer of "zooish" care, the slaughter has continued at just one remove and with the added incentive of the high price a live Orang will fetch in any part of the world. Before long, a *healthy* captive adult Orang could be worth up to £2,000 delivered in U.K. or U.S.A.

In the main body of this book, my wife tells of what we (mainly she) tried to do towards developing a *new* approach to Orangs. In the process we have come to have other ideas, and perhaps a better understanding, of Orangs as our intimate and infinitely lovable associates.

I do not want, here, to pick upon anyone in particular. But I must admit to deep shame whenever I come home to Britain from Borneo, and see what is done in the name of public education (for money) at the greatest British zoo, prototype for the world.[1] Look, for instance, at their great Sumatran male Orang. Here he, and before him his predecessor "Sandy,"[2] have been under-employed and overfed into a condition of horrifying and humiliating monstrosity. Yet this sort of thing satisfies deep urges in that part of the human ego which brings humans to zoos and causes them to confine the strong. Nowadays a veneer of apparent kindliness has to be overlaid, but fundamentally the approach is not distant from that of the medieval bear-pit.

[1] The high rate of Orang mortality in London's old-fashioned ape-house was constructively discussed six years ago in *The Times*. No improvements have taken place.
[2] See p. 171.

DEAR COUSIN!

In the Orang's Bornean homeland, conduct considered normal in western zoos would be unthinkable. Among most Dayak tribes the two deepest taboos are against incest and ridiculing animals. It is very widely held that anyone who laughs at an animal—or in any way puts it into a position of humiliation or contempt—thereby endangers not just the welfare, but the very *existence*, of the whole community. The penalty for making fun, even of fish or frog, is "petrification," turning into eternal stone through hail. In some parts of Borneo all the rocks, knolls and caves are considered due to this abominable conduct, in the ancient past.[1]

The fact that such a captive ape—there are others in exactly the same plight in Pretoria, the Bronx and elsewhere—sometimes cannot even stand up (let alone get a stand) pales into insignificance beside the prestige, and thus public pennies, that such a giant attracts. The biggest Orang possible is a public excitement. Good people take their children to inspect, at close quarters, his unmoving, noiseless torpor of despair.

Pitiful too is the plight of the many young Orang put behind treeless bars.[2] There are very, very few who can hope to survive for a normal (wild) life span. To an Orang—as we shall see—there is dim hope where there is no tree, no butterfly, no flea!

Orangs love and live for trees (though they have never seen a coconut palm), leaves, mucking about, investigating, worrying, irregular rhythms, natural jokes. This also, roughly, underlies my attitude to my dear wife. But though I love her as life itself, there have been times, in recent years, when I have wondered who was living with whom. She with me—or Derek and Ossy? I with her—or with Nigel at the shaving soap? She tells only half of it. Honestly; but only half. Still, that is the way intelligent women do tell things. Intelligent feminine Orangs, like our Eve for that matter, as well . . .

[1] For details on the very important part this belief plays in living thinking see, for instance, my account of the upland Kelabits in the book *World Within*, London, 1959.

[2] See Chapter, v.

On my limited observation, there is not much to choose between ape woman and woman woman in some ways. In another way, the best contemporary writer to have visited Borneo put it, civilised style, in his *Cakes and Ale* :

"I stopped and put my hand on his arm. 'You must know that she was deceiving you with all your friends. Her behaviour was a public scandal. My dear Edward, let us face the fact : your wife was nothing but a common strumpet.' He snatched his arm away from me and gave a sort of low roar, like an orang-utan in the forests of Borneo forcibly deprived of a coconut, and before I could stop him he broke away and fled."[1]

[1] Somerset Maugham, in Borneo, 1927-8.

I

Orangs in the House

The lack of direct contact by speech is
not a fatal obstacle to a sympathetic sub-
jective understanding of behaviour in
man or animal. There is no need to go
to natives in foreign lands—we only need
to consider our own babies and tiny children. We cannot cross-question them,
and yet we can to some extent understand
them.

Prof. Dr. Heini Hediger,
Zürich, 1955

THERE IS NO TRUE FEELING OF CHRISTMAS IF YOU LIVE in the tropics. Time and rhythm of seasons get lost in constant warmth and sweat, unchanging sunrise and sunset, green trees and bright flowers for ever in your garden. Often while dating letters in November or December, I wonder how it would feel, now, to sit in front of a fire, to watch rain-drops run down a window-pane or have an icy wind torment my ears while I walked over hills or along shores, hands deep in pockets.

Christmas Day in 1956 started rather badly. I had retired to our bedroom with a bad cold, an excessive supply of medicine and a mood. In the back of my mind hovered my elderly Malay *amah*. She would do nothing unless I got up and told her what to do with the turkey. Tom was sad, as always when I was sick, and I had to get well quick. The cats at least made me feel that this world was still good: Miau lay on my chest, sleeping, her head resting sideways over her paws. She was pregnant and heavy, but I could not bear to move her. Mini, her daughter— like Miau with black and yellow patches on her white fur and a straight tail (rare in Borneo)—lay in a round rattan basket at the side of my feet. She nursed her litter of three, purring.

Dozing under the buzzing fan I was suddenly startled. Tom burst into the room:

"I've brought something for Christmas," he said and a ball of chestnut red fur fell on the bed. "A baby Orang-utan for you, a male."

I sat up and the little thing wriggled itself into my lap, its arms groping at my sheet and pyjamas. It was a beautiful baby with wide dark-brown eyes in light-coloured sockets, a small nose like a triangle with a velvet skin and a broad mouth with soft, sparse hair like a young boy's. His body and long arms and fingers, his short legs and long toes were covered with hair, hard and shaggy. On top of his head this hair was sparse and upright, framing the face and the small, human ears with a halo of sweetness.

"His mother was shot. He was found by a Forest Guard in a long-house," said Tom. "We will have to look after him for a while. How shall we name him ?"

"Bob Inger is coming to-night . . . what about 'Bob' ?"

"Good. I hope he will be flattered—I will tell him right away when he comes. Will you be all right ?"

Bob Inger, Curator of Reptiles in the Chicago Museum of Natural History and an old friend, had come to Sarawak to observe and collect reptiles. He was studying the reptile collections in the Sarawak Museum: countless bottles packed full with snakes, lizards, frogs, turtles. He also relied on the Museum for skilled help and field transport.

"He will be here soon . . . to discuss his trip," said Tom, "you better get up if you can."

Yes, of course ; but first the baby. He was perfectly happy in my arms. Would he take milk ? Surely he was best fed like a human baby ? Where could he sleep ? Would he try and get away ?

I put him down in an arm-chair, taking his arms and feet away from my body. When I left the room to look for some things to make him a bed, a piercing scream called me back. Turning I saw he had climbed down and started crawling towards me. I took him up and he was instantly quiet. Obviously this was needed : to cling to mother !

We have been living in Kuching, the capital of Sarawak, for some years. This is a town of 40,000 or so, until recently very quiet, even "old-fashioned". A dream-town of the old eastern style, with a Chinese core. Narrow streets lined with open shops, packed with merchandise : baskets and mats, candles and joss-sticks and dried octopus hanging from the ceiling ; large earthenware jars, packing-cases and sacks all over the floor, with displays of onions, duck's eggs, birds' nests, dried fish and sweetmeats. Under the counter in glass cases are soap and tooth-pastes, combs and fancy jewellery and behind this shelves with beer and milk, pots and pans, piles of Cantonese plates and bowls. Crammed into the background darkness is a large round table where the family takes meals, squatting *on* chairs. A bowl of rice for each member and a large dish or two in the centre from which to pick what is wanted with chopsticks; a bit of chicken or fish, leaf, mushroom, prawn, egg, cucumber.

Along the Sarawak River is the market. This is a space of concrete under a large shingled roof, packed with stalls displaying fruit and vegetables: coconut, banana, pineapple, water melon, lemon, pawpaw, orange, lettuce. Some are new: durian, roseapple, jackfruit, mango, rambutan. And there is a large variety of vegetables.

You sit down on a bench in a corner and ask for a cup of coffee. This will be hot and sweet, the small cup of thick earthenware filled to the brim and spilling over into the saucer; you are allowed to drink from either or both. The market is always full of people—Chinese, Malay, Dayak, Tamil—shopping, choosing, selling, sorting, carrying, looking, gossiping, offering their wares with their scales ready to hand. Others sit quietly beside their stall, reading a paper.

A small corner is taken by Indian curry-sellers. A selection of bright yellow, mustard, orange, dark red, and brown dough is spread on green leaves, different mixtures of spices kneaded into large balls. From each, or some, a small bit is taken according to taste, wrapped up in a leaf and bound with twine. From here you can step into the fish-market, where the sellers will greet you with loud cries, offering the great catches of fish from the estuaries. Prawns and crayfish are piled on tiled counters; crabs in large baskets. In the next stall only pork-meat is sold (to non-Mohammedans). Chunks of fat and meat dangle from large hooks, and live pigs, bound up in round baskets, lie patiently in the shade. Farther on, fowls are sold—chickens, ducks, geese, pigeons. Take your pick, peeping through large round baskets.

Beyond this centre of buzzing activity, which also includes the post office, customs sheds, courtroom, the Resident's office, secretariat, and the other official buildings, lie the Malay *kampongs*, the Chinese and less numerous European bungalows, dotted about along roads lined with trees and telephone wires.

Our house, tucked away behind the golf course, is on a small hill, at Pig Lane. A steep drive curves up sharply, with small space to turn on top, a shed for the car and Land-Rover. Walking along the *dapor*, a low wooden building housing the kitchen and servants' quarters, you enter the house over a few wooden steps. A narrow passage is lined with Dayak swords and hats, crammed over black, white and yellow monsters painted on the walls by up-river visitors. Coming out into the main room—a vast open veranda looking over the garden with low rails all round—lady visitors of orthodox tastes often exclaim, "How can you *live* here ?" Others, at best, remain silent, scanning the room with awe.

For this is the housewife's bad dream, a conglomeration of things Bornean, pinned and stuck on wall and ceiling, lying on tables and floor everywhere and nowhere : war hats and feathers, shields and swords, old bead necklaces, shells and dragons, statues, Siamese buddhas, plates and wooden carvings, drums, ceremonial sticks, Ming jars, masks, baskets, mats, *tapa*-bark coats, fine sarongs, Rhino horn, hornbill ivory, Birds of Paradise ; and on every free inch of table piles of books and papers, neatly arranged by their master in sections of planned activity and interest where no one may touch them, even to dust.

The confusion is also carried into the bedroom next door. This looks over our garden, which is a sloping green wilderness of fresh, broad banana leaves, tall durian trees, and pineapples growing in the tall grass. There is a small lawn with frangipani and red hibiscus and a forlorn wild rose in a large dragon-jar. The "gardening" tends to be sporadic. Tom often walks here, dressed in a sarong and deep in thought.

A small study on the other side of the house is lined with books and untidy cupboards. A filing cabinet, always overflowing with papers, and a desk under the small window, leave only a little space for the mat of split bamboo on the floor. After journeys into the jungle or to the sea, even this is often covered by unpacked suitcases. "No room to put things away," is the excuse.

This house and its contents have grown over the years. Nothing may be altered, taken away, chopped off. It has grown to fit its master, his ideas and fancy, his work. It is a living thing; and all that comes from outside has to fit in somehow or go away if it cannot do so. You either love it or hate it.

Bob had to fit in somewhere: outside at first. We walked round the house to find a good place for a cage where he was sheltered from the hot sun and monsoon rains. A small roofed platform, leading down from the bathroom to the garden, seemed ideal. All that was needed was to connect floor and roof with tall wire and to add a few shelves, a swing and ropes, and a box for the night. We put a wire-window into the connecting door, so that we could see him from the bathroom.

Walking about with him I felt his small body hot against mine. I began to worry, for I had heard of baby Orangs dying rapidly of pneumonia and colds. Was this little thing in my arms perhaps ill and needing immediate attention? I had no idea how it had been kept or by whom, and there was no way of finding out during the holidays.

In a panic I packed Bob into the car and took him to the Veterinary Officer, whose new building had just been completed in the outskirts of town. Osie Merry dealt mainly with pests and problems of domestic animals. He was at home. Bob was relaxed. Like a good child he bore patiently Osie's nudging and poking.

"He has a slight cold," he said, "and you must not worry about his temperature. Perhaps his runs higher than ours. I'll give him an injection against tuberculosis. That will be a safeguard."

Back home I weighed him on our bathroom scales: 15 lb.

His milk teeth were white and fully developed. "About a year old," said Tom. "We must weigh and observe him regularly. Look here, I will give you some cards, and every day you observe something special you write it down and keep it on file. But you must *really do it*, don't just say 'yes.' Promise me to do it, because you can never remember these things correctly." I promised.

2

Bidai was a lad of fifteen when he first came to Pig Lane. He had a broad cheerful face, his full lips curved up at the corners in a perpetual smile. His black straight hair was cropped short, shining and somewhat gluey under a film of coconut oil. His father, a wiry old man, was headman of the large Land Dayak long-house under the slopes of Mt. Poi, a high mountain clothed in virgin jungle fifty miles to the west along the monsoon-swept coast. The most important animal here was the turtle.

Across the sea from here, and not far off, lie the two Turtle Islands, Talang-Talang Besar and Talang-Talang Kechil. Sometimes, on a bright day, they seem to float like clouds over the water, on a horizon where the blue of sea and sky melt into a belt of haze in the distance. But the glistening white beach, with a hump of green jungle behind it, soon hurt the eye on approach. Here the huge Green Turtles come up at night, heaving and sighing, to lay.

Sleeping in a hut right over this beach, as we often do, it is strange to wake at night to hear the "thump-thump" of turtle flippers working away at the sand. Often I pick my way in the dark of a starlit night to follow the Malay watchmen patrolling the beach, marking the nests, quietly.

It is essential to move slowly, not to betray your presence by movement and shadow. For as long as the great beasts move up from the edge of the sea, until they are ready to lay, they are easily disturbed and turn back into the water.

They make their nests in the sand, digging out craters with their strong flippers in quick, regular movements—periodically resting to breathe and sigh deeply. After working for an hour, a narrower deep shaft is dug with the hind flippers into the compact and moist deeper layers of the beach, the "secondary nest." Into this over a hundred eggs are laid, falling down from the ovipositor, one by one every few seconds, a gleaming mass of soft, white ping-pong balls. Then the nest is covered—the shaft first—the hind flippers padding and pressing the sand firmly down into place. To complete the task, the whole site is then laboriously disguised with further digging, flinging of sand, and slow movements away from the nest—and finally towards the sea.

During the summer months of the "laying season" (they come all year round, but like June to September best), over ninety turtles may come up in one night on one island, crowding and disturbing each other's nests. The nests are marked by the watcher with a numbered flag as that turtle lays. And in the early morning the small beach looks like the bulky back of a bull wounded with banderillas.

Before the sun is up, the men come to dig out the eggs. They squat down and shovel the loose sand back with both hands, bending forward as they feel their way deeper and deeper. Suddenly, they bring up handfuls of eggs, filling basket after basket, counting and recording each nest as they work. Sometimes at this hour a turtle is still left on the beach, ready to go but still working hard in the broad daylight to disguise what has already been taken.

A harvest of up to a million eggs and more goes to Kuching market every year and is eagerly bought as cheap and delicious food by Malay, Dayak, and Chinese. But though a large percentage of the eggs are taken, the turtles themselves are sacred. They must not be disturbed, or touched ; and once a year *semah* offerings are made, prayers chanted and rites performed on the islands themselves to make them come in great numbers for another year, to lay.

Bidai's father, Nimbun, is the Grand Master, the *tukan*, every year for this *semah*, the fertility rites. He makes himself a uniform for the purpose, a blue coat of ancient army style with epaulettes and stripes in gold and red, which he wears over a loin-cloth. Nimbun is a distinguished friend of ours, and when he asked us to take his son away from the remote long-house, to see and learn a little in town, we naturally agreed.

First we took him to the islands, while my husband was busy there transplanting the regular quota of eggs into protected sections of the beach for hatching and rearing. Here, after six to eight weeks buried under the sun, a hundred or more tiny turtles at a time burst up from the sand, madly flipping to get away towards the sea. Here they are first put into sea-water tanks, to protect them from sharks, crabs and snakes inshore, until they get hard and strong enough to survive these dangers. Then they are taken by boat into deep water, where they swim swiftly away, not to return till many years later, when they are full grown and come back to lay.

Bidai had to learn the hard way, starting with the job of trying to understand. He spoke only Land Dayak. He was (like many Land Dayaks) rather frightened of not being able to please or of doing wrong. Small tasks like washing a dish or cooking a fish, though easy at home now seemed difficult : might not the new "father" like it done differently? Might he not eat the bones and leave the flesh, have salt in his tea or sugar on his rice ?

As everywhere with young people, comfort and fun, so essential in strange surroundings, came from a friend. This was another boy called Ina, slightly older than Bidai, a little deaf, serious, intelligent, with whom he had shared his childhood in the village. They were always together, discussing each new task ; learning the *lingua franca*, Malay ; shooting migratory waders along the beach, then learning to skin them properly with an exciting equipment of tiny knives and scissors, cotton-wool, arsenic, needle and thread—though it took them some time to learn to label their specimens properly.

36

Eve, inside her night-sack

Eve learning to walk, aged 1

So they both came to live with us in town. They wanted to buy smart shorts (or, better still, longs), shirts and tie, a radio, to become government servants with a regular salary (Bidai now earns £25 a month); to have friends of different races and backgrounds, to go to night school; and for the holidays to go back to their village, big men.

Bidai, especially, soon showed a wonderful talent for looking after live animals. He was patient and loving and steady. He cleaned Bob's cage, spoon-fed him his milk three times a day and gave him his fruit. Every afternoon he took him into the garden and played with him on the lawn for hours.

The job was easy at first. But soon there was more to do: a second baby Orang arrived. It was a female. We called her "Eve."

3

Eve was brought in by a forest guard in a small basket from the country behind Lundu from the Indonesian border, where Orangs still occur in the jungle. Her mother shot, she had been taken and brought up in a Dayak long-house for a few weeks. Sold to a Chinese trader nearer the coast, she had been kept on a chain under his house, like a dog, fed on bananas and biscuits. When the story got round—as stories always do in a country where gossip of queer and extraordinary things is one of the universal pleasures—the Forest Department confiscated the animal and brought it to us.

She was much smaller than Bob, very thin, and her neck was sore and infected from the chain. She had a full dentition, but her weight was only 7 lb. She refused all food except bananas, which she nibbled slowly and daintily. Our Malay *amah*, Dayang, who had brought up, over the years, a crowd of children and adopted children, looked her over with suspicion:

"She is surely small, Mem, she must take milk or she will die—let me try and take her!"

With a sigh of relief I handed her over, hoping that Dayang at last had found what she missed so much in our household: a baby to cuddle and look after. In her view, a house without children was no house, empty, without purpose, without fun. As the years went by, she stayed on with us in spite of this defect, hoping against hope. Similarly, grateful to her faithful service over the years, I refused to see that she could not see well with her one eye, hoping against hope. For the house was often too dirty: cobwebs and dust accumulated freely, which she would take away with a broad smile when I pointed them out. An ideal relationship!

Eve refused to drink and Dayang registered despair:

"She will die, Mem, you will see!"

We made a new cage for her alongside Bob's. Bidai put a comfortable little nest in it with blankets, wood shavings and leaves. We placed her inside and she crawled away, hiding from the cruel world, apathetic.

Next morning, I made up my mind. With a glass pipette I forced milk into her. After some spitting and coughing, violently trying to get away, she took it; slowly first, hesitatingly. Then I changed over to the baby's bottle and she really drank. The first battle was won.

Bob was by now fully established in his cage next to the bath-room. Seeing Bidai from a distance working in the kitchen early in the morning, he always whined in anticipation of his milk, screaming hysterically if Bidai disappeared from view, only for a moment. He took his cup, clasping it firmly with both hands on the floor, bending down with pointed lips, sucking the milk slowly and noisily until nothing was left.

His cage was easily washed down every day with a hose and brush. Bob knew perfectly well that he had to take the same treatment, but he would always try to evade the issue by swinging up to the highest shelf, from which Bidai had to pull him down. Then he submitted, his thick fur glistening under the running water, his eyes shut tight in patient suffering, lips protruding to catch a drop or two until the wash was over.

The early morning sun fell straight into his cage with a warm glow. Within ten minutes, his fur dry, his body warm, he was ready for the day's activity, for food and fun. We soon discovered that he liked to play during all hours of the day with leaves and branches, twisting and bending them, peeling bark, poking for insects, carrying them about. The routine order for Bidai was to cut fresh branches every morning for Bob and to put them in his cage.

As we got up he always looked fascinated into our bathroom, pressing his little face hard against the wire-door. The master shaving, the mistress combing her hair—all details of human toilet delighted him. My diary reads:

"7.3.57. Bob now knows how to bang on wire screen as counterplay (teasing).

Phases: (1) hanging from rope, wildly banging; (2) face to wire, squeezing; (3) squeezing and blowing raspberries; (4) rapid twirls on rope, slaps on wire with hands and feet, often grinning; (5) lashing at wire with rope as well as self, raspberries and all."

It took him two months to learn from phase 1 to 5, mildly incited by Tom. His relations to me were quieter. He liked to sit on my lap, better still to walk about in the garden clinging to me, and protesting violently when the walk was over.

After his first meal of fruit later in the morning—varied according to season—he was busy for a long time with his branches. He often made elaborate constructions, using his shelves or box as support and tying branches and ropes, even the whole of his swing, into one enormous tangled mass. He would then sit on this, satisfied, scratching and fussing, sometimes dozing for half an hour in the midday heat.

A second pot of milk, with a handful of soft rice mixed into it, was served at noon. After sipping the milk he usually took the rice into one hand and shovelled it into his open mouth. A shower of rice grains would go astray, right over his face and body, sticking to his eyelids and ears and all over him. The next hour or so he usually spent picking grain after grain from his hair and from the floor of his cage.

His feeding habits seemed wasteful—he only took the very best bits of fruit and leaf at first—but after a while he came back to the bits rejected earlier. So that, although he had fixed feeding times, three of milk (and rice) and two of fruit, he was busy picking at something or other almost all day long. If not at fruit, leaf or bark, then at his cage, a loose bit of wire or plank; any weak shingle in the roof was quickly detected. His door, too, was constantly worked on, and by endless fiddling—rather than deduction—he sometimes managed to get out.

One night Tom and I were dressing up to go out. This we both hated, though for different reasons. For him it meant a stiff white shirt constricting his broad neck, soaking him in perspiration even before the game of the night was on, hated socks forced into narrow shoes, and worst of all, the sudden discovery that trousers and cummerbund were once again too tight. I was just getting out of the bath when a roar for immediate attention sent me flying for needle and thread. Soothingly, I knelt down to see better with needle poised.

"Bang!"

Something heavy had fallen on to the living-room floor next door. Without stopping to think I dashed out with not much on. And there was Bob with a Ming jar in his hand. He held it triumphantly over his head staring at me—and I at him. A heavy bronze mirror (Chou Dynasty!) lay at his feet. Slowly I walked towards him gazing in a trance at the jar.

"Bob . . . my darling . . . come to your mama . . ."

As I took the jar from his hand he, delighted, climbed on to me. Tom stuck his head through the door. A broad grin appeared on his face.

"I always knew the stories about Orangs stealing maidens are quite untrue! I think it must be, I suspect . . . the other way round!"

Next morning poor Bidai was working laboriously with hammer, nails and wire repairing the cage. With Bob looking on, delighted.

Every afternoon we took both Bob and Eve for an extensive outing in the garden. Usually Bidai and I took turns. Once released from his cage, Bob would race away madly, turning head over heels across the lawn. Sometimes he would dance about, standing upright for a second or two with his feet well apart; then, waving his arms like a windmill to keep his balance, he would stagger a few paces or walk in a semicircle, giving the impression of a drunken, bear-like dance. His usual way of walking, however, was on all fours, arms supporting head and shoulders, fists close together under the body, feet moving behind, slightly spread, lurching and shuffling along.

Eve was taught to walk also. Bidai or I put her down on the lawn and walked away ten yards. She usually screamed madly, feeling abandoned, then (still screaming) started scrambling towards us. We then moved slowly away from her, keeping a distance. Soon she was so occupied with the task of walking towards us and controlling her limbs, that she forgot to scream. After a while she walked quite well and started to explore the garden on her own if we sat down with her. But she never ventured far; if we were out of sight for a moment, she always started screaming.

Bob only took a mild interest in Eve. He felt her face, hands and genitals; poked at her; smelt her, once or twice tried to play, mostly by biting her belly, gently. After "accepting" her in this way, he usually dashed off to investigate the garden which he found more interesting. The pineapple patch was one of his favourite grounds. There he pulled the leaves with his strong teeth, biting away half-ripe fruit. He would poke for ants and other insects—and, in the ground, for earth, which he chewed with relish.

One of our turkeys, which roam freely over the garden,

once made her nest in a thicket of pineapple and grass. Bidai built a leaf shelter over the nest so that she should not sit in sun or rain. Her name was Pauline. My diary reads :

"15.11.57. Bob discovered Pauline to-day . . . he went as near as he dared. Pauline hissed. Bob looked at her for a long time. Then started pulling pineapple leaves to frighten her. Pauline hissed intensively. Bob now started to rattle the poles of the leaf shelter, also pulled leaves—now Pauline hissed still stronger, with all feathers on end. Bob did not touch Pauline, and came away when called, without fuss."

Usually Bob got very dirty every afternoon. Like good children, both he and Eve had to submit to a thorough weekly wash in the bath-tub. After the first shock—they did not like a lot of water, nor too cold—they both delighted in the bath and insisted on carrying away a towel or flannel. Then they sat in the cage, with proud looks on their faces, placing towel on head or draping it round the neck—to tear it to pieces afterwards (as their reward). At night they were given a sack each, for comfort and warmth. After receiving their evening meal as the sun went down, both crawled right into it—to go to sleep usually curled up on one side on the floor of the cage. Bob often snored slightly. Neither ever stirred before sunrise.

4

During the first few months of her stay with us, Eve got terribly spoiled. Bidai and I cuddled her as much as we could to encourage her feeling of well-being. She was taking her milk regularly with delight, and slowly gained in weight. Her hair grew long and shiny. Every morning she sat in front of her cage door, basking in the sun, whining (if someone passed) to be taken up and walked about. As long as she was so small and sweet, it was easy to do anything with her.

But she remained very delicate and I was constantly worried about her health. I had no experience of raising babies and often consulted mothers on what I should do. At one stage Eve contracted worms; we took her straight to the clinic and from then on we checked her regularly, and Bob too.

Eve had a distinct tendency not to foul the "nest" in her cage, where she slept at night (and often for half an hour or so during the day), but crawled away from it. When clinging to me she was usually clean. If the necessity arose she always lifted her small, pointed bottom away from my body, but she was less fastidious with strangers, and I never handed her over without an appropriate warning.

During that time I read a report from San Diego Zoo, California. Here an Orang baby had been born in captivity, a female, Noëll. I wrote to them about our Orangs and asked for information on weights and diet, their experience in general, and on whether it was possible to educate them to cleanliness. Back came a delightful photograph of Noëll showing her in a baby's play-pen, clad in nappies. O land of a thousand possibilities!

Mrs. Alloway, who looked after her, wrote:

"No, I didn't have Noëll "house-trained." I think that would be very hard to do. Every time I changed her diapers it seemed as though she waited until I had put a clean one on her then immediately soaked it. I washed diapers galore every day . . ."

Though Bob and Eve grew rapidly, gaining about one pound a month, their steady progress and increasing strength was deceptive. Orangs are the slowest growing apes; their development to maturity takes roughly ten years. It is closely related to that of a growing child. If they spend all their childhood in captivity, it becomes impossible for them to survive on their own, in the jungle. There were two possibilities: either to try and educate ours to jungle life or to let them grow up to become zoo-animals.

In spring, 1958, Bob was about three and we often discussed

43

what should become of him. Somehow we felt that he had
adapted himself so much to living with us that it would be very
difficult, if not impossible, to teach him new ways ; and we were
not certain how this could be done. With us he seemed contented
and happy, very unlike the Orangs we had seen in some zoos
in Europe and elsewhere : sickly, pathetic, hairless, lethargic
creatures doomed to boredom and close confinement for the rest
of their lives.

Our own. facilities were too limited to keep Bob until he
reached maturity. If he was going to be a zoo-animal, it was
much kinder to give him to a good zoo now, while he could still
adapt himself easily to new surroundings. The picture of Noëll
in her nappies at San Diego—she was exactly Bob's age—stayed
in my mind as a ray of hope. In a place where Orangs bred in
captivity in a near-tropical climate, Bob might find a home
where he could continue to be a great ape. We suggested him
as a future bridegroom for Noell (but many years would pass
before he could start a family of his own), and San Diego
accepted, delighted.

But before all was arranged for his transport—by sea to
Singapore and by air over the Pacific—something else happened.
We received *three* new babies, all males, in quick succession.
This really brought matters to a head !

The Conservator of Forests, as Game Warden, was much
concerned. He confiscated any young Orang kept, sold or otherwise found in human care in accordance with the Game Ordinance.
Anyone shooting an Orang in the jungle—and the only way to
capture a baby is by shooting the mother—or keeping or selling
a baby committed an offence, punishable by fine. But in the vast
jungle areas, especially along the Indonesian border where
Orangs still occur, effective control was (and is) a near-impossi-
bility. It was always difficult to establish the real offender and
prove his guilt. In some cases, the animals had been taken into
Sarawak over the border, from Indonesia. This complicated the
legal situation, for it was impracticable to apply Sarawak laws in
such cases. Fines were not heavy enough to out-balance incite-

44

ment given by illegal traders, who often paid large sums for a baby.

Experience had shown that Orang babies kept in long-houses or private households as pets only had a slight chance of survival. They died in a matter of weeks if not protected against *human* diseases, and not given the right kind of food. It was important to save every Orang, so in recent years no private person has been able to obtain a licence in Sarawak to keep an Orang as a pet. There was an unwritten agreement between the Forest Department and the Museum that confiscated babies were given to us and that we should bring them up as best we could. No one else was interested.

So we had to start devising mass methods of rearing them, now. Perhaps it was even possible to find new ways of keeping them, in a half-wild state, so that they might be put back in the jungle later ? If this could be achieved at all, it would be a long-term project. As it stood, we were faced with three new little creatures, entirely helpless and depending on us. We decided to name them in honour of those people who were most concerned in the cause of Orangs.

The first was "Tony." "Tony" stood for Sir Anthony Abell, then Governor of Sarawak, who soon afterwards appointed a commission to make a census of the Orangs that survived in Sarawak's jungles and to submit recommendations of what could be done to protect them more effectively.

The second was "Frank." "Frank" was for Frank Browne, then Conservator of Forests in Sarawak and Game Warden. In this capacity he was the legal protector and stepfather of all Orangs.

The third was "Bill." "Bill" had his name from an old friend, Bill Smythies, author of *The Birds of Borneo* and an Assistant Conservator of Forests, since made Conservator.

Tony was the smallest. He was very sick and skinny, his little body covered with boils. He was found in this condition, in a Dayak long-house where he had been kept for some time. Although he was less than a year old—his fang-teeth were just showing—he refused to cling and lay curled up in the improvised cage which we had quickly made for him. His arms were perpetually crossed behind his neck, his knees were pressed to his belly. It was agony to see him thus; he seemed to have lost all interest and joy in life. When I showed him to Osie Merry he said what I already felt: "I can treat him—he has pneumonia —but I don't think it will be much good. And perhaps it is better for him to die; he will never be a healthy animal."

We treated him and he responded. But when he was rid of his cold we found that he was infested with worms. We treated him for that—and he started a new cold. After an agonising fortnight, during which I could hardly bear to see him suffering in his cage, he died.

Frank and Bill were healthy. Both about a year old, they were placed together in a large new cage which we had made for them. They were given a swing and ropes for exercise, leaves and branches to play with, blankets and sacks to cuddle. Their cage was put next to Eve, whom they eyed with interest. From here they could also peep into the kitchen, so see all day long what was going on.

Bill had been sold for as little as five Straits dollars (about 15 shillings) to a Chinese trader. Frank had been found in the forest, by a forest guard, sitting over the body of his dead mother, whining. Her body decomposed, and it was impossible to establish the reason for her death. Little Frank, who had been without food for several days when first found, greedily took the bottle. Bill followed his good example without difficulty.

Eve was very jealous of the new-comers. She had always had this tendency, but as long as she was the spoiled baby there was not much reason for complaint. The two new babies, much smaller than her, got a lot of attention from Bidai. Looking on crossly from her cage, she protested furiously when she saw him cleaning or feeding them. She sat on a high shelf, glaring at the babies, whimpering. If no notice was taken of this, she started to climb wire and ropes, up and down, in a frenzy, crying, and often banging her fists. She lashed the wire with the ropes to attract attention and was even jealous of Bidai when she saw him with me, talking together ! Although she was over two years old at that time and quite strong, she did not romp and play in the garden with the same exuberance and vivacity as Bob. After a period of exercise she always came back to cling to Bidai. He did not encourage her, though he was flattered.

Though the babies infested our lives from morning till nightfall, and the household seemed often out of gear because of them, we could hardly bring ourselves to see Bob go when the appointed day came. He went, escorted by Ina to Singapore, where he was to be looked after in transit by the Veterinary Officer. Then he was to fly to San Diego, the whole journey taking a week.

Tom could not bear to see him off. I said good-bye to him with Bidai on board ship at Kuching and could not help the tears running down my face. I was not ashamed because Bidai understood.

But soon we had a telegram announcing his safe arrival, and later a delightful letter from Dr. George Pournelle, Curator of Mammals at San Diego Zoo. He wrote :

"The day Bob arrived at the Zoo he was placed in our hospital for routine check-up and quarantine. During the same evening I received a phone call from Barbara Kadas, our nursery attendant saying that our new arrival was taking his cage apart. When I reached the hospital he was just pushing his head through an opening that he had made by untwisting a strand of the heavy link. He had already shoved out his blanket and several toys that were in the cage—evidently with no intention of returning. When he saw me he evidenced no sign of anger or frustration, but simply held out his arms to be picked up. The cage was repaired and strengthened and he was returned. The next day we discovered him diligently working away at another opening he had made in the top.

Bob was next confined in a larger, more sturdy enclosure in the hospital yard where he promptly went to work again, coming out during the night and forcing an opening in another cage housing penguins. Here he was found by his keeper in the morning. No attempt had been made to harm the penguins. We then decided to place Bob temporarily in a heavily barred cage that had been recently used to house a big grizzly bear and had also, in the past, held lions, pumas, and other large animals. Next morning he was found in the hospital feed-room where he had spent the night dining sumptuously on bananas, apples, grapes and other goodies. He had patiently worked one of the cage bars loose, more a case of skill than strength.

Bob is always gentle and never displays temper when dis-covered—simply seems to shrug philosophically and lifts his arms to be picked up and cuddled. In spite of (or because of) his tendencies he has already become a real personality. However, we believe he could have more aptly been named Houdini."

Evidently, Bob missed the home comforts of Pig Lane—where he never broke out on the town—even in San Diego. Presently he was settled with his little mate "Noëll" and they became a happy, well-adjusted pair. He featured on TV also with great success, for he was very co-operative.

After extensive repair to Bob's now empty cage next to the bath-room, Eve changed quarters. Seeing her little face peeping into the bathroom helped to get us over the sore emptiness after Bob had left. Though this cage was larger and allowed more freedom to swing and climb in all directions, Eve did not like the change at first. She complained, whimpering, making scenes. It was not difficult to understand that she did not like it and wanted to be taken back to her old quarters. Crying furiously, she hid under a sack for several hours when we took no notice.

Next day she got over it. Stimulated, she accepted the new ropes and swing, carried all the leaves and branches given to her to the highest shelf, twisting and bending them into a tangled mass. Carrying up the sack between her strong teeth also, she finally sat on the whole construction, satisfied, looking down.

Bill and Frank also settled down well. In October, 1958, they weighed sixteen and fourteen pounds. They spent much time wrestling and chasing each other. Bill, older and stronger, was quiet, and very greedy. Frank, a real buffoon, liked to snatch bits of fruit and branches from under his nose, often taking in good grace a punch for his teasing. Though they liked to bite each other's necks, fingers and toes, they never hurt or were nasty to each other. If one was taken out of the cage, the other complained bitterly. At night they cuddled in one sack, often embracing each other.

One day when we returned from a trip up-country, the cages seemed bare : there was only one branch in each one. Tom was furious and called Bidai.

"Why have you not given some more branches ? Surely you can see that they have nothing to play with ? What do you think you would do in a cage with nothing to do ? Think ! Are you mad ? "

"Tuan . . . there are no more branches . . ."

"No more branches ? Look around ! What are these . . . and these up there . . . and there ? Cups and saucers ?"

He was nearly in a frenzy now : "Thank God this is what we have plenty of in this country, trees and branches, miles and miles of them ! I don't care where you get them or how high you climb. That's your business !"

From this day on, Bidai climbed higher and higher into the trees every morning to cut down plenty. He did not use a ladder. A *parang* between his teeth, he swung up easily, using his strong arms and bare feet to grip the bark, vines and branches. The Orangs from their cages looked on, sympathetic.

Perhaps we were wrong and should give them more freedom. Perhaps *they* should learn to climb high and live in the trees. Was it possible, in this way, to bring them back to where they belonged, to a natural life, once they were strong enough to look after themselves ? But when was this ? Bob, at three (and 35 lb.) had still been a playful baby, though strong. Was he, at that age, depending on a mother to teach and protect him in the jungle ? Or on a group of playmates to feed, fight and wander in the right way, and, reaching maturity, to breed a family of his own ?

There was no book which could be consulted, no field report anywhere available describing what we wanted to know. We had to try and see for ourselves, in the jungle—and then by further experiment at and around our home.

II

Orangs in the Jungle

The history of behaviour study is at
root the history of the struggle against
the deeply seated tendency in every
human being to humanise the animal.
Even the biologist must carefully guard
against the intrusion of anthropomor-
phisms ; the more primitive the man,
the greater his humanising tendency. He
humanises—i.e. demonises—not only
animals, but plants and even completely
inanimate objects as well.

Prof. Dr. Heini Hediger,
Zürich, 1955

Afternoon in the garden. *Above*, Eve stays close to Bidai, while Bob is busy with some fruit. *Below*, she looks to Bidai for protection from Bob's alarming hug

Eating was Bob's principal occupation

GAUN ANAK SURENG IS THE MUSEUM'S STAR COLLECTOR
and taxidermist. An Iban Dayak from the Sebuyau area in the
Second Division of Sarawak, he had come to Kuching as a young
man to look for experience and work. It is a tradition with these
people to go for long journeys as young men and see for themselves the world outside their native villages. After months or
even years away they will return, full of stories and sometimes of
riches. In the old days there were head-hunting expeditions,
tribal wars or rhino-huntings. Nowadays they go to work in the
towns, rubber-tapping, timber-felling, or to the oil-fields on the
coast. Or simply to visit their tribal relations all over the country
along the great rivers, with trips over the watersheds into the
deep interior far across Indonesian Borneo.

Gaun, very much an individualist and outdoor man, a keen
hunter, had travelled all over Borneo under the auspices of the
Museum, had accompanied scientists and collectors, university
expeditions, nursing them along over weeks in jungle camps or
long-houses, lending his keen eye and quick hand without fuss.
An ornithologist in his own right, he knew the birds of coast,
lowland and mountain. His skins were immaculate. And he
knew how to mount specimens, preparing them in the way he
had seen them alive in the jungle. The Museum in Kuching is
full of his work.

He was now middle-aged, still tall and slender, and had grown
a moustache (this took a long time) since coming back from
Malaya. Years ago, after a clash of personalities with the Curator,
his boss, he had resigned from the Museum and joined the
Sarawak Rangers for special training in jungle warfare. He took
part, as many other lads from Sarawak, in the tedious war against
the Communist partisans who terrorised wide areas of Malaya
over several years. After serving with distinction, he came back

to Sarawak and re-joined the Museum. He wanted no other job.

At first, Gaun was sent on his own to find out the best areas for observing Orang-utan. His diary of over a month's travel now served as a guide. As Tom could not go himself, he decided that I should go next with Gaun to look after me. I went to the Museum to see him. He was working with rubber gloves and spirit bottles.

"Have you heard ?"

"Mem ?"

"It is arranged that we go soon ?"

"Mem !"

"We shall take Ina also. He will look after the *barang* (food, clothing, bedding : luggage, in fact), and will you take your equipment as usual ?"

"Mem."

"I shall have my camera and some papers also, which I will pack myself. Shall we start early, at seven ?"

"Mem."

"By the way, don't worry about food. Perhaps, if you take enough rice, I will bring tins to share for the three of us . . ."

"I shall have my gun, Mem."

Though relieved to be able to get away from the office work for a while, I knew that Gaun was not too keen to go with me. I sympathised with him in a way, but it was too late to change my sex. I was not worried. We had been on trips before. These had been archæological expeditions, where I had worked with a team of Museum people, mostly Malay and Dayak, sharing a large camp in the Great Caves of Niah—including Gaun, then on a related but separate collecting job. We could converse in Malay, easily enough. I knew his wife and child, his showmanship, his occasional outbursts of hypochondria. All would be well. . . .

Back home for a frenzy of packing : the camp-bed, mat, blanket, pillow and mosquito net wrapped into a raincoat for the night. Three changes of old shirts and trousers, a battered cloth cap, a spare pair of gym shoes ; towel and sarongs for bath, change and sleep. Soap and toothbrush, yes. Books, no. But a small battery of essential medicine ; and, most important, torchlights and mosquito repellent. Now for the food: a plastic bottle for tea, a cup, frying pan, kettle and pot. One spoon perhaps, yes. And a knife. And to the telephone for an order of tins from the Chinese trader in town :

". . . twenty tins of bully beef . . . twenty tins of sardines . . ." —tea, coffee, sugar, biscuits, condensed milk. To round off, cigarettes and a secret bottle, to keep the lads quiet. For the rest we would see what we could do on the way.

Early next morning I took leave of Tom.

"Ina, you will look after the Mem well ?"

"Yes, Tuan."

"Have you got everything, Gaun ?"

He stood there in smart jungle green, woollen socks tied over his trousers with string (he did not like leeches), gun in hand :

"Tuan !"

Before leaving, I went to see the children and poked my hands through the wire of their cages.

"Good-bye, kids," I said, "I'm off to see your cousins in the jungle !"

2

For three days we had been travelling by boat, first over the South China Sea and then up-river, into the Sebuyau district. The last night we had spent in a Dayak long-house near Plai ; there we had found a local Iban guide, Bakar, to take us into the forests where Orang were reported seen recently.

All morning we had been walking in single file : Bakar first, followed by Gaun, myself and Ina as tail. Through a maze of secondary jungle, rough, thorny thickets, sometimes wading shallow, muddy streams ; or crossing an open field of *ladang* grass in sizzling heat to plunge back with relief into the shadow of trees and undergrowth. In this type of forest—which grows up within a few years, on soil claimed by Dayak planters for one crop of hill-rice by felling and burning virgin jungle—going is particularly tiresome. Thorny undergrowth and creeping vines take more than their share of space, once the domineering high trees are felled. Not even years of re-growth can restore the balance.

The way seemed too long. Again and again Gaun and Ina had cut away thorns and bushes with a swift flick of their parangs to make it easier ; had given me a hand for balance over slippery tree-trunks felled across a stream or gully ; had pressed a long stick into my hand (quickly cut on the edge of the narrow path) to help through muddy water, where the eye could not see where the feet were. But they pressed on. Since early morning we had made only one halt—sitting under the tall trees and smoking a cigarette.

Bakar had said that sometimes, during the fruit season, Orang came quite near the long-house. There were a few now, in the high jungle near Bukit Plai where we were going . . . perhaps. I had drunk greedily from my bottle of black tea, which dangled invitingly from Ina's shoulder-bag. I was too tired to inquire, to talk. Now I was soaked in perspiration ; and still we were going on. We came to the edge of an open field where green blades of young rice grew over and amongst an untidy mass of burnt, fallen tree-trunks. In the middle, a make-shift hut on high poles with a roof made of dry leaves.

"We can camp here," suggested Bakar, "and also come back for the night. There is nothing farther on."

A notched pole led up to the house. The simple plank door was secured with a single bamboo diagonally across. We went inside to sit down with relief in cool darkness, on the swinging bamboo floor : this was heaven ! Off with the shoes, hats, bags and camera. All that we needed was there. In a corner, the hearth of dry loam with a few sticks of firewood. A broad plat-form of bark to spread the mat for the night. A few baskets covered with spider's-webs. A *jala*, throwing-net for fishing. A few dirty cups and enamel plates, battered and gay, rusty nails on the rafters and a wire to hang things to dry. Water ? Of course, there it was outside the door—in an earthenware dragon-jar with a bit of split bamboo as pipe for the rainwater to gush into it.

Within a few minutes, Ina had made a fire, put the kettle on, and placed the pot of rice (cooked earlier in the day) on the floor. Gaun produced a bunch of sweet, juicy jungle fruit from his bag, and Bakar went to fetch a few broad green leaves for plates. I opened a tin of meat and put it alongside the rice. Then we sat down in a circle, cross-legged.

The best way to eat here is with the hands. The rice, sticky and firm, is taken in small lumps between the first three fingers with a kneading movement, picking up with it bits of fish, meat, or vegetables and sauce. You bend slightly over and down for mouth and fingers to meet above your leaf-plate. Rice is the main staple food of all Bornean peoples ; they eat a great deal, usually three times a day. Fish and meat are luxuries, to go with it in small doses ; some people may have them only occasionally. But of rice you must always have plenty, even if poor, and enough to give to visitors and relations as well.

The meal over, we had a cup of steaming coffee. Happy and refreshed we lay down, taking the bags for pillows. Now it was time to plan the rest of the afternoon—how to go on. . . .

At the edge of the rice field the virgin jungle stood, a tall, dark wall of green against the clear, blue sky. The light bark of the nearest giant trees, now unprotected, peeled off in the scorching sun. From here the jungle spread unbroken towards Bukit Plai. We would go, two by two in a wide circle to meet uphill, looking for the nests of Orang-utans.

Though long past midday, the blast of heat hurt us as we left the cool darkness of the hut. But now we were light. I scrambled through the field to reach the shade with Gaun, who carried my camera and his gun. Bakar and Ina disappeared amongst the trees. We were in the jungle.

Silently, lightly, we walked along under a dome of green, the screaming of cicadas in our ears. Young growing trees, tall and slender, stood sparsely under the shelter of giants. Here and there, less vigorous trees were being strangled by vine and fern. Creepers swayed down from the dimness overhead. Wide, tissue-paper butterflies sailed gracefully by. Below our feet the ground was a soft carpet of humus as we scrutinised the greenery above us for signs of life.

We walked for a long time, Gaun ahead of me, bending down small branches every ten paces or so to mark the way. Sometimes he disappeared from view and then I would look anxiously for these limp, upturned leaves. Suddenly there was a crash, and I noticed a large branch swinging. We stood stock-still, and then I walked up to Gaun.

"Red Leaf Monkey," he said quietly.[1]

I had seen nothing living.

Now we began to climb up a ridge through wet, dark-red boulders, half covered in moss and fern. Moist and cool, they were the haunt of snails and giant ants. A red millipede curved its spineless body and multiple feet in a wavy dance ; on touch, it went suddenly limp, then curled up into a ball. Leaf and stick insects blended their bodies against leaves and branches. Small lizards breathed heavily, but stock-still. Birds were few, but varied; squirrels, frogs of various kinds. We heard the harsh screams of far hornbills and presently the swishing of their wings overhead. A busy woodpecker worked away somewhere, drumming.

We had no view from the hill-top, as there were high trees all round us. Gaun stood under one, waiting. He pointed to the forest floor. It was covered with empty fruit-shells.

"These have been eaten by monkeys, perhaps Maias," he said, grinning. "I have once seen maias eating these. They are called '*buah kubal akar arang*.' " We collected a few, together with some leaves from the same tree, and made a note of the date and location. This is necessary for later identification: there are over 2,500 species of trees in the tropical rain-forest.

[1] *Pygathrix rubicundus*, a true Leaf Monkey, often mistaken for Orang.

Once more the sudden crash of heavy bodies jumping off and scrambling away into distant trees. This time there were three or four and I had seen them: long-tailed Macaques. They eyed us for a while from a tree, before walking slowly away along the high branches. Gaun and I sat down to wait for the others. We discussed the result of the afternoon. We had seen no nests. Gaun said there was not much point in going any farther. There were not enough trees in fruit, and if Orang were about at all there would have been nests. Then, from the distance came the high yelping and barking of dogs. This was the last straw: hunters!

Gaun stood up, facing the direction of the uproar to let out a single, piercing "U-u-h." The call came back, and soon four people emerged through the trees with as many dogs which dashed about madly, their tails waving. Two Iban hunters, barefoot in battered shorts and shirts, with small baskets on their backs, *parangs* at their sides, and guns dangling from string over their shoulders. Broad, dark smiling faces, muscular bodies. The others were Ina and Bakar.

We sat down to talk and offered them cigarettes. They had been after wild pig all day, but had been unlucky. One of them was the owner of the hut. We asked if they had seen any signs of Orang; they had not. Presently we started off on the long walk back, first laboriously explaining that we wished to *see* and observe, not to shoot. A shade of darkness, a murmur of wind in the crown of the trees above, announced coming rain. Perhaps we could make it before the downpour came? We walked quickly now, downhill. Tired, once falling over a root, I scrambled on, trying to keep up with the men. As we neared the edge of the forest the rain, hissing and drumming, came on over us like a tide. At last, as we made for the hut over the open field, it caught us and soaked us to the skin.

3

The men had gone off into the rain, wrapped in towels, for a bath in the nearby river. Too tired to bathe, I simply hung up my soaked shirt and trousers and changed for the night. The meal over, we sat round a tiny oil-lamp. The dark sky was lit with stars and a pale moon hung low over the horizon. Mosquitoes buzzed through the open door of the hut. For the third time I smeared my ankles and wrists with repellent. I was too tired to be irritated. Nearly asleep, I listened to the men's talk; it was about Orang-utan.

"Once," said Bakar, "I was walking along the Pedawan stream. I heard a fearful sound of 'muh-muh-muh' not far." His face, contorted in an effort to imitate a low staccato grunt— eyes shut, lips pointed—looked ludicrous in the flickering light.

"Ah, that is Maias," Gaun confirmed. "I have also heard this sound."

They discussed why it sounded like that.

"I have heard it in the evening on new and full moon," Bakar suggested, and this appealed to the others.

"Yes, and when they make this sound they usually stand up, on their nests. I saw it clearly once."

He told more about Maias—how human-like their behaviour seemed, how clever they were at spying things from afar, silently moving in the trees.

"Even in sickness," he said, "they are much like us." He spoke slowly, often repeating a sentence in a different way to underline what he meant. "They often suffer from fever—what we call *alar* [periodical attacks of elephantiasis], during the periods of new and full moon—and then they live in their nests for three or four days, making a sickly sound."

The men were now sharing dark, loose threads of Siamese tobacco from a bamboo box, rolling long, thin cigarettes neatly into nipah-palm leaf.

"They are never afraid of us," Gaun related. "Once I was walking along the upper Emplanjau stream and I saw three of them." He was sitting cross-legged, his sarong wrapped over his bare shoulders and legs, like a sack. "Their movements really surprised me : they moved fast, from tree to tree and did not stop, like monkeys do when they see human beings. They were *Maias kesa*, the small kind."

But Bakar did not quite agree.

"Although our people are often frightened and dare not go near—because three were assaulted once in the upper Sebuyau— we say that *Maias kesa* are not dangerous. They run away when they see men, especially if they carry guns !"

"But their teeth are just as strong as *Maias rambai* and *timbau*, the larger kinds," the hut-owner, a tall man with shining gold teeth now spoke for the first time. "You can see it clearly when they shell fruit and peel bark off the *Empetir* tree. They never stop and move on until all the fruit is eaten."

He got up to shut the door of the hut.

"I always respect them," he said quietly, "and I think of the old times when they were much more numerous."

From outside came the rhythmical "tok-tok" of a night-jar.

"My grandfather used to tell me—that was in those times when we were still in the Sadong River—the old stories of how man and Maias came to live in the jungle."

Here Ina, the Land Dayak, spoke up—last, as usual, in the Land Dayak way. He told them a long story, the legend of a woman and her son who lived in the jungle with the Maias, the Orang-utans. It ended thus :

"The Maias, and his wife and their son *refused* to return and follow them to the village because they were beasts and did not like to live with human beings. They wished very much to return to their old home in the deep old jungle. So that night the Maias, his wife and their son gave very much thanks. They said that they were sorry that they could not mix with them any longer because they were beasts. Kumang and her son now went back for the first time to the village. The Maias and his family stayed a while in the hut. When the padi and other kinds of food were finished they returned sadly home to their own house in the very deep old jungle, where until to-day the Maias always dwells."

Gaun—never the perfect listener—was restless. He delved among his kit in the back of the hut, looked outside, lit his small hunting lamp and took up his gun.

"What about this pig?" he suggested. "I should like to go now with the moon down."

Bakar agreed. "We can try along the river, and the other two through the forest. We might have a good chance."

They got up and quickly changed into their wet shirts and trousers. Ina looked at me inquiringly.

"You can go, Ina," I said. "I shall sleep."

I watched them go—scrambling down the notched pole and walking away in a file into the mist that now hung over the rice field. The booing call of an Eagle owl came from a mile away.

Feeling my way in the darkness, I crawled under the mosquito net. My legs ached. Oh, to lie down, to sleep! I was alarmed for a moment by the rustle of rats or mice in the roof overhead, but not for long. I fell asleep.

4

No pale midsummer night, no dark mornings here, at two degrees over the Equator. The first rays of light (shady grey) crawl over the sky before six in the morning. It is quiet then. The frogs have ceased; birds and cicadas are still asleep.

I was the first up and outside. I did not relish the idea of more walking. Perhaps we would walk for days, weeks even, without any result? I washed with cold water from the dragon-jar, ladling it out with a coconut shell. Then it was the turn of the men.

They were already busy. Gaun was laboriously skinning the result of the night's hunting. No pig, of course, but a large fat black civet. They had seen its eyes gleaming in the light of their hunting lamp. A large pot with rice was bubbling on the fire—enough to last for both the morning and midday meals.

"I did not hear you come in last night," I said to Ina, foraging in my bag for a dry pair of trousers and shirt. "Were you late ?"

"Not very. We only went for a couple of hours." He helped me to roll up my mat and pillow and fold away the mosquito net.

"Shall we take all the *barang*," he inquired, "or do you want to stay here for another night ?"

I consulted with Gaun and looked over the map. We could try in this district for one more day, on the other side of Bukit Plai, and leave the heavier parts of our baggage behind, to be picked up later.

If this was unsuccessful we would have to try a different area altogether.

The hut-owner was sitting cross-legged on the floor, getting ready to go home to his long-house. He held a pocket-mirror with one hand in front of his face, with the other a pair of rusty pincers. With the pincers, he picked at some sparse hair sprouting on his chin and cheeks. Then he combed his hair, slowly. Even here men suffer in the early mornings to please !

We sat down for a breakfast of rice and biscuits. Gaun gallantly gave me the civet's brains and liver, which he had fried with a taste of onion and garlic. They were really due to him as the hunter ; but he felt that they must go to the most honoured person in the hut !

"I had a dream last night," I said, munching, "about Maias." Bakar's face lit up.

"What did you see ?" he asked keenly.

"Oh, nothing much . . ." (I had chased them madly but every time they had got away when I tried to touch them.) "I don't really remember. But I saw them quite clearly, swinging in trees, looking down at me . . . perhaps 'muh-muh-muh-ing,' " I added, jokingly.

Something was wrong. Bakar's face had fallen.

"This is bad," he said, "this is very bad."

I looked at Gaun inquiringly.

"People say," he explained, "that when you see something in your dream that you want to see during day-time ; an animal, a man you are looking for—if you see this someone or something in your dream you will never be lucky. It is no good to go out and look in the morning. You may as well stay at home."

He smiled. But Bakar was serious.

"You may as well stay here," he told me, "or go pig-hunting."

"Let us pretend, then," I said smugly, "that we are pig-hunting. Nobody will notice. We had better start soon."

I gave some tins of meat and fish to the hut-owner, thanked him for his hospitality and wished him luck. Then we went off, for another jungle day.

There is something wise in this dreamworld of jungle-men, a philosophy of live and let live, hunting and being preyed upon : it *is* important not to be too keen. If you are in a hurry or frenzy, if you try and force an issue, it is no good. Often the nightmare expresses a wish hidden away, an anxiety about what you want to achieve. It is better to stop, think and do something different for a day.

In the old times before Christian missionaries came to Borneo, the Dayak peoples inland lived in a world animated and ruled by spirits—good and bad. They strictly observed omens and dreams. Their life and welfare, farming, their wars and migrations thus depended on chance meetings with birds and beasts in the jungle and on the interpretation of dreams rather than "common sense." Now they have widely accepted a new faith which gives a chance to get round these inhibitions with good grace. But the tradition of taking them seriously and putting them into practice where it seems reasonable or successful, remains. The rule—not to follow up what you were looking for in a dream the night before —is one of them.

We were unlucky all day and achieved nothing. Not a trace, not an old nest even, all around the slopes of Bukit Plai. We went back to Pendawan, and next began working the upper Tuba stream.

Much of the old jungle in this area had been cleared, more than a hundred years ago, for farming land. We found the site of an old long-house made by the early settlers, people who had fled when the warlike Saribas and Skrang Dayaks had invaded the country. Some of the tall poles of iron-wood, the ancient pillars of a large long-house, stood still upright amongst the overgrown jungle trees. Foraging among the leaves at the foot of the poles we found the ground littered with broken porcelain— Chinese and early European. Mapping the site and taking samples of the remains in the ground was a routine task for us, a valuable addition to Borneo's archæological map, which dates back to the earlier beginnings of man in the Great Caves of Niah to the north, over 100,000 years ago. Any evidence of trade and migrations, of long-house architecture in the more recent centuries adds factual knowledge to the folklore and traditions of the people themselves.

Scanning the trees as we had done for days, we were delighted to see that some of the high durians, planted here by the early settlers, were in fruit. This was hope. For the durian—a spiky, heavy fruit the size of a football—is favourite with Orang-utans. The trees are usually very tall with sparse foliage, over 100 feet and hard to climb. Dayaks and Malays live in their durian orchards during harvest time, collecting the fruit when it falls with a heavy "thump." It fetches a high price on every Asian market—in spite of a strong smell which is penetrating, and painful to western noses—reminiscent of rotten eggs, onion and bad meat. It comes in seasons—twice a year—and long before you get to the market you know when durian is on: the whiff is terrific. Prospective buyers make a business of choosing the right one by feeling it; turning it round and round carefully not to be hurt by its sharp spikes; smelling it closely; and by judging colour—it turns from light green to golden yellow in ripeness. Inside the thick and hard shell, which opens into sections like an orange, grows soft, pulpy white flesh over large hard seeds. This is delicious and juicy—if you ignore the smell.

Gaun pointed at a high durian and I followed his arm. "A nest," he said. "You can see it is a few days old."

About thirty feet high in a fork, was a tangled mass of broken branches loosely folded together into a broad platform. The leaves were green, but limp.

"In a new nest the leaves are still fresh," he explained, "they turn limp after two or three days."

We went on, careful not to make a noise, looking and listening, spying for a glimpse of other colour in the dense green foliage overhead. We saw another nest, its branches fresh; about twenty feet up, partly hidden from view.

"We better wait," Gaun said quietly, "to see if an Orang is inside. You cannot tell, if you try and see from directly underneath."

It was about midday, very hot. We sat down, contemplating the nest. There was no sign of life. I tried the field-glasses: nothing. After about ten minutes and still no movement I took my camera, walked up to the tree to take a photograph. As I was pointing the exposure meter to read the light my hand froze in mid-air. A scrambling and rustling, a barking sound came from the nest. Then a great body, clad in dark, shaggy, chestnut-red fur moved away into the dense foliage. My camera forgotten, heart thumping, I stood gazing stupidly at nothing but leaves. Gaun walked up to me.

"You have disturbed him in his midday nap," he said. "We better not follow but show him our good intentions. He will be in a temper now."

5

Gaun insisted on a durian meal first. He had found a fallen fruit, cut it into sections with his knife and offered me of the pulpy flesh. I had a hard time with the stuff, trying to keep my nose shut and look pleased. We had gone back to the long-house site, where we had left our things and where we would camp for the night. Presently Bakar and Ina met us, their eyes shining. "We have seen many nests," they reported, sitting down to share the meal, "about half a mile away from here—and three *Maias kesa* moving in the trees."

Quickly we made a plan for the afternoon. We would go in a wide detour, roughly approaching the nests from behind, driving the animals (if this was possible) towards our camp where there were some more trees in fruit. This might give us a chance to observe them at dusk and dawn, without being visible to them ourselves.

But first the camp itself. We chose a spot, under a medium-sized tree with dense foliage. Bakar and Ina went off to collect palm, vines and other broad leaves for a roof. Gaun started cutting saplings for floor and rafters. Within half an hour a rough shelter was ready to take equipment and camp-beds on a platform of sticks, a few inches off the ground. This—for protection from the many crawling things—and a roof for the rain, was all that was needed. And a cooking session to prepare the meals of night and following morning. Because if we were at all lucky and near the animals, we could not afford to make a fire, to make a noise later. Finally, we disguised the whole camp with branches. Perhaps we could deceive the Orangs in this way and see without being seen. With luck, rain—or the durian—might take away the human smell.

We walked in pairs, all afternoon. My legs, now getting used to steady walking, did not hurt any more. Light and with ease, full of hope in our excitement, we were driving in the direction of the camp, nearing the nests. We had seen many birds, the lair of wild pig, a pair of giant squirrels playing and chasing high up in a tree, waving their bushy tails in sudden movement.

Gaun saw them first: two Orangs—no, three, in trees about a hundred yards away. They moved, half hidden in foliage. We got nearer, creeping under cover of branches, to see better. Oh, to be able to climb a tree silently without effort, to swing up to them, look at them properly! One of them stood on a high branch, with one hand interlocked higher up, the other hand taking one spray after the other that sprouted outwards from the main bough, turning them inside towards his face, to chew the young tips. He was about three feet tall, with a pouch of fat under the chin ; his movements were systematic and relaxed. The back of the other animal was partly showing, his long fur spreading down evenly, like a Dayak war-coat, from the top of his head to his legs. He stood erect on twisted branches, legs spread apart, holding on to a vine. Scraping away industriously at the bark of the tree, he poked a finger right into it, now and then peeling it with his teeth. He was roughly the same size as the first, but looked less fat. The third was hidden, high up in the crown of the tree. It was his movement that had betrayed them all. He was using the branch he was sitting on as a swing, trying to get within reach of a branch farther away. Soon he moved over. Under cover of the loud rustling of branches as they received or were left by the heavy animal—he did not jump as monkeys do—and we came a few steps nearer. Now we could see the first two clearly.

"*Maias kesa*," Gaun whispered, "the small kind."

Although the Dayaks group Orangs into three kinds—*Maias kesa*, the smallest ; *Maias rambai*, the medium ; and *Maias timbau*, the largest—no such distinction of races by size is possible. The broad cheek callosities to frame the face develop with maturity, more or less defined. They have caused early observers to believe in a separate race in Borneo distinct from another, with leaner faces. But the cheeks depend on sex, age and state of health ; they occur in many variations from a size slightly noticeable in young animals and females to enormous formations in old, well-fed males.

As males often reach twice the weight of females and are distinctly larger in height, it is not difficult to recognise a pair of grown-ups when seen together. This group of three were young animals of approximately the same size, the one with the large pouch probably male. It was possible that such teen-age groups,

68

Orang country. *Above*, a dayak long-house. *Right*, the skull of a large Orang, revered by the dayaks as an ancestral spirit-hero

Left, Gaun searching for Orangs in the jungle. *Above*, an Orang's nest, a tangled mass of broken branches 30 feet above ground which perhaps form regularly at a stage when the young leave their mothers to fend for themselves, were called *Maias kesa*; and that the regular occurrence of such groups of distinctly small animals has caused Dayak observers to believe in a separate (third) race and to give them this special name. Gaun told me that he has often seen them in groups of three to six, never a *baby* amongst them. He said that the difference between *Maias rambai* and *Maias timbau* is in over-all size. *Timbau*, the largest (also called "*Maias pappan*") has always got the broad cheek callosities too. Both, declared Gaun, occur in smaller groups, mostly two or three together, often including a mother and baby.

Judging from Bob, who was past three when he left us, these three were about five years old. The two nearest had now started to play in the tree-top, climbing up with great speed, trying to outdo each other until the top was reached. Finally one crashed down on the other, swinging madly on a thin branch he was holding. Then they both climbed over to the next tree. We followed them carefully. One was standing in a rattan tree completely overgrown by vines and epiphytes. He scraped around in a hollow from which he shovelled and hurled away wet leaves and humus. He inspected orchids and fern, holding them close in his hand under nose and eyes, and then sent them flying to the forest floor. One of the others looked, sitting close; then joined in the game. Once he took what the other held out in his hand, hitting and grabbing it with swift movements of the arm. The other rushed forward, snarling. But that was all. They went on with their business like two small boys digging away industriously in search of hidden treasure.

Soon they moved on. Often they stopped, peeping down to the ground. They seemed to drive steadily in the direction of our camp and it was hard going to keep up with them. Looking upwards as I moved along, I did not notice the stump of a young tree, which had been cut off with a *parang*, poking through leaves on the forest floor. It caught the tip of my shoe and I fell headlong. I heard a deep, short bark; looked up. He stood on a branch on all fours, eyeing me, rattling his perch, grunting.

"Careful now," I thought. "Big Brother is watching you."

I stared at him, he at me. Prostrate awkwardly on the floor, I must have looked a sight from his perch. He threw a twig at me, then moved slowly on. I got up to brush away ants that were biting my neck. I was deeply ashamed, *malu* as they say in Malay (an important word with deeply proud people). What a stupid thing to do !

"They are moving towards the camp," Gaun consoled me. "We had better stay here, not to frighten them off."

He collected leaves and fruit of the trees our friends had been feeding on : *Empili kukut, Empili pai, Berangan* nuts, *Pensi.* I wrote up my notes on what we had seen. It started to drizzle. It was important to try to make contact with them again before they retired to the nests we had seen, or decided to make new ones somewhere else, at sundown.

Slowly we returned to the camp. There we met the others. They had observed one large Orang—the one I had disturbed in his midday rest—and had seen him feed on durian roughly in the area where we had found him at midday. Perhaps it was better to try and contact him next, as we knew the location of his present nest. It was probable that he would return to it for another night.

At six, half an hour before sundown, we were on our way, walking towards the old one's nest. The drizzle became steady rain which dripped down on us through the ceiling of leaves, running over our faces. For a moment it crossed my mind that Gaun might object to go on in this way ; that he might wish to sit down, to be dry, to stop. But I need not have worried.

"I think the Maias may want to retire quickly in this weather," he said with feeling ; "we will have a good chance of getting near without being seen in the noise of this rain !"

We approached the nest in the same way as in the morning, careful to remain under cover and not to be seen from above. Then we saw him. He had a bough between his teeth, walked with it on a high branch towards his nest. He got in, feet first, holding on to a branch that stood out from the nest, like the handle of a frying pan. He took the bough with both hands, lifted it for a second over his head and placed it inside the nest, turning the tips of the leaves at the end of the branch innermost. He got on top of it, padded it down with strong, regular movements of his fists. He sat down, looked in our direction. I gazed at him—had he seen us? Apparently not. He lifted one of his long arms overhead, scratched his back. I suddenly felt the mosquitoes tormenting me; perhaps it was the same with him! But I did not dare to scratch.

Then he was off again and reappeared, after two or three minutes, approaching the nest from the same high branch as before. He carried a durian, holding its stem between his teeth, the large spiky fruit dangling in front of his chest. "Tuck for the night," I thought. "What a good idea."

He placed the durian in his nest and went off on a new errand. As he climbed away, however, the fruit fell down with a big "thump." He stopped dead, sat down, looked down, contemplating this new development. But he went on, after four or five seconds, in the old direction.

He came back with a new branch, placed it inside, folding it underfoot, sat down. Then he bent forward in sitting position and started to pick away at loose bits of leaves that stuck out at the sides and from under the sitting platform. He snipped them off with his fingers, placed them inside under and around his body, turning slowly in a circle. Sometimes he took up a branch a second time, lifted it, turned it round, and replaced it differently. All his movements were slow, steady and deliberate. He gave the impression of having a distinct idea of what he wanted—a comfortable sleeping-place.

It was getting dark. He had been busy for fifteen minutes. Now he sat quiet with his back to us, one hand interlocked in the "handle branch." It was difficult to distinguish his body from the dark foliage in the background. His nest was exposed to the rain with only a light cover of foliage higher above. He scratched, picked at something or other in the nest, and turned to face us. Then he lay down, disappearing from view. We could only see his hand, still grasping the branch that he had used for getting in and out. One elbow appeared, to scratch and move a branch once more. We sat still for a long time, while the forest grew dark and the mosquitoes danced around us with their irritating high-pitched hum.

There was no more movement. We were cold. I was thinking of my Orang children sleeping in their comfortable cages at home, wrapped in sacks. Was it possible for them to come back to the jungle, to build nests and sleep in the rain ? Slowly feeling our way in pitch darkness we crawled back to camp, to the dryness of the small roof and the protection of the mosquito net. We did not make a fire or light a lamp. Bakar and Ina knew just where to look for the three young Orangs in the morning. They had located the nests which they had made before dark. We would go and see them before the sun came up.

6

Sleeping in the rain in the jungle—a few inches off the ground, the blanket of the dark lit only by fire-flies—is difficult for anybody not used to it. The eyes, though longing for sleep, open wide with each noise reaching the ear : a sliding, a rustling in the leaves, the call of a sleepy bird, the flutter of a bat, the howl of a what ? . . . something rattling at the cover of the cooking pot ? You reach for your torch to pierce the darkness with a ray of light—but it is nothing. A quick search around the bed to make sure (there might be a snake !) and back to close your eyes for sleep. As it slowly carries you away a new noise starts up : a frog or toad, it must be sitting right next to you with its uproar of deep, rhythmical quacks. Or is it only a cricket in the hut pole ? Comfort and a feeling of security finally comes with your companions round you.

Grateful for their presence, and for the small roof over our heads, I lay thinking. Each of us, though in different ways, would be unfit for a life in the jungle. I myself would perish within a matter of a few days, if left on my own.

My three companions would last for some time, but they, used as they are to community life and a uniform diet, would not be able to survive thus for ever. Even the nomadic Punans, a Bornean tribe that lives scattered about in the jungle areas of the deep interior without agriculture, depend on trading with the outside world; and, most important, on their own society, as all humans do.

Our friends, the Orangs, are close relations. Seeing them in the jungle feeding, at play, or building a nest, they seem very close to us indeed. It is quite a different thing to look at an Orang through the bars of a zoo; that is like looking at a man in prison or in a mental institution. You get a distorted idea, a kind of thrill, or perhaps you just think it funny. But here in the jungle looking at them as they go about their business, seeing their minds at work—you *understand* them because you can see that you might live in that way, if you had to live wholly in jungle.

First of all, the trees. They are safe. We had just built a platform of sticks, as a matter of course, for ourselves to sleep on —because the forest floor was unsafe, uncomfortable, and wet. Similarly the Orangs had taken to the trees and devised a way to live in them by building nests, sleeping platforms, for the night. And as the tropical rain-forest—their world—once stretched unbrokenly over this island where they came to live, was it not natural to stay in the trees which held all the food they wanted, instead of coming down to the floor to meet the discomfort and dangers of another animal world!

Their huge arms and their short, strong legs with feet almost equal to a second pair of hands, were now suited to a life entirely in trees; there was no need to walk on the ground. Their minds, similarly, had taken to the trees—for here you can best develop a mood of slow, relaxed contemplation and curiosity. Any danger or intruder is seen from above before it sees you, which gives you plenty of time to decide whether it is worth making a row. If it is not—well, then it is nice just to look! The old

Orang, when he had sat in his nest looking down and scratching his back, had seemed to me like an old woman looking down on a busy boulevard from her window on a summer evening. It is nice to *have* a view, especially if you don't have to do much about it. But think about all the things men even *do* to have a view. And think of the delight of children in climbing trees and making a "home" or "hide-out" there for themselves!

But even if you have a thick fur to keep you warm, to let rain-drops run down without touching your skin; even if you have strong teeth to show your strength, to carry things with or to use as a universal tool—even so, jungle life is tough for a slowly developing animal. An Orang must *learn*, for many years, how to survive. Completely helpless at birth, it depends entirely on its mother at first for food, protection and warmth. Then (within two or three years perhaps ?) one must learn to do things for one-self. The next stage is to get away from mother, to live with companions, to establish a place in one's own community, by way of peck-order, and to become strong; to learn the ways of tree-life and to wander over great distances in search of food. And, after ten years, one starts a family and a new cycle with a life of one's own making.

The babies that had come to us were in their helpless stage, when they still entirely depended on their mothers. Being adaptable and intelligent animals, they had accepted the human being as suitable substitute mother and started to learn and live in a *human* way. Was it humanly possible for humans to teach them the *ape* way—so that they might be fit to return to tree and jungle life ? Contemplating my miserable anxieties and fears under the small shelter in the rain and darkness, I could not help being doubtful. Though, being human, it is fairly easy to *under-stand* the ape way, to feel them closely related as beings, as minds even, we live in fact very far away from their way. We have organised our lives and dependencies in such an intricate way as to become useless in their jungle world. I felt that unless *I* learned to live like an ape first, it would be impossible to teach an ape baby.

74

With the ridiculous thought—had I not missed the bus, so to speak, thousands of generations ago ?—with the strong desire to become an ape-woman, I dozed off into sleep. The rain fell, the platform of sticks with the beds presently stuck out from a pool of water. Ah, well, to be sleeping in a tree, listening knowingly to the noise of the jungle, relaxed and at peace, as if perched in the box of a concert hall !

"Mem . . . Mem !"

Something at my shoulder. I stared into darkness.

"Mem . . . wake . . . it is one hour before sunrise !"

Ina held a cup of tea in front of my nose. Cold. Cold and wet all over, teeth chattering. What was I—what the hell was I doing ! —in this misery, in the dark ? Trying to be funny ?

"Gaun . . . my camera . . ." I saw it, in my mind, floating in a puddle of water. His face loomed up.

"It is all right," he said soothingly, "here, in the metal box, under canvas."

The rain had stopped. A dew had settled on us, on our things. To get out and going was good.

"Gaun . . . we better all of us try and see the Small Ones. I want to take pictures. Two of you must help me to get up into a tree . . ."

Yes. To get into a tree. This was the first step, for me. . . .

The request to get into a wet tree in darkness was the craziest ever of crazy wishes which people like Gaun and Ina got used to accepting without fuss. I admired their patience, their steady, helping hands as they heaved me up. They could have refused, have said it was impossible, dangerous, foolish . . . but they didn't. Slowly, careful not to miss, not to be too noisy, we wormed our way up a high tree full of vines and creepers.

It was standing close to a durian in fruit and to the tree where the Orangs had their nests. These stood up, spaced in

75

different heights, as dense, dark blobs of foliage. I selected a position half-way up, about twenty feet high, with what seemed to me an adequate view into the nests. On a high branch as far as I dared outwards, in a fork, where there was enough foliage to hide my presence. Gaun lashed me up.

"You better go away, all of you," I whispered to him, "they will not like it if three of us remain here." I thought for a moment, uncertain what to do if something unexpected happened. "Just leave me a *parang* and some string to tie up my equipment."

"I can hide myself well . . ." Gaun hesitated, tying one more knot for safety, "I will tell the others to go but you must let me stay near you, Mem." I could not refuse.

"All right," I whispered, "but not too near."

"Don't worry," he started along my branch towards the main trunk. "I want to see also. . . ."

I settled as best as I could. The sky faded into pale grey behind the world of dark leaves ; leaves dripping with the rain of the night, leaves over and under me. Straining the eyes into the nearest nest, I bent over some of the twigs that were in the way. Swinging gently on my branch, I was ready for the sun to come up, for the Orangs to wake. Slowly the light increased, but there were still no colours. One of my legs was already stiff, with an irritating tingling from toe to thigh. I eased the pressure by putting my hand under it. But it was no good ; it stayed limp.

Soon I could see more. There, the nearest nest slightly below, stood up in a fork, a mass of bent branches. I strained my eyes into it, unbelieving first—but there was no doubt : it was empty ! No dark shadow, nothing inside. Not even a little bird. It was a nest all right, but empty.

Mad with disappointment, I examined the other two. One was higher than my perch, I could not quite make it out. Nothing showed above it. The third was farthest away, and lower. I snipped off a few more leaves, to see better. But this one *was* occupied ! I saw a dark body, back turned slightly upwards under a covering

76

of twigs, feet folded under the belly. One hand was tucked under the shoulder, the other gripped a branch that stuck out from the nest.

The first rays of sun touched through the roof of foliage, smoothing away the wetness of the night. Leaves, orchids, vines and ferns exhaled a faint mist that floated upwards. There . . . a rustling sound, a movement in the farthest nest . . . he had turned over.

A delightful spectacle followed, the *Grande-Levee* of jungle-man. He sat up, looked about, scratching his back. He lifted his elbows sidewards, fists rubbing the eyes ; inhaled deeply, stretched his back straight and flung out wide, first one fist, then the other, to each side. Slumped back, exhaling. Sat, to look down over the edge of the nest. He scratched his back between the shoulder-blades, slowly but firmly, again and again. He stretched once more, this time bending and straightening his legs ; sat for a while gazing, as if contemplating the new day. Then he started to poke around inside his nest.

A rustling now came from the high nest. I looked up, delighted : it was occupied after all ! And soon it was clear that there were two in this one as more than two arms moved, scratching and stretching. I could hardly believe it, yet it was the simplest solution, the easiest explanation of the empty nest : the two others had slept together, in this miserable rain, hugging each other for warmth.

Soon they got out and slowly climbed across to the durian tree. It was 6.45 a.m., breakfast time. There was no sound. No squeak, grunt, nothing. Yet they seemed to be in intimate contact with each other.

Two got a durian with the first go. They bit off the stem from its branch, supporting the large fruit from below with their hands. They then moved farther away, carrying the fruit between their teeth. The third and smallest Orang made a mess of it. He bit the stem, wrenched and twisted it carelessly without supporting the fruit from below. And down it fell, to land on the ground below. He stared after it, then looked up to find another and went to get it. He was careful now and finally swung back to hang on one arm, hugging the fruit between hand and feet in close embrace.

The two others were now poking the shell to find out where it would split. Now and then they sniffed their fingers, holding them close to their noses. Finally, they wrenched the shells open, tearing and splitting with teeth and hands.

Their hands plunged deep inside the fruit and came up full of white pulp, which they stuffed into their mouths. They munched, blew raspberries, smacked their lips. Their lower lips often protruded wide while they inspected what they had got in their mouths. They went back repeatedly to pick more fruit, and ate until they could eat no more.

One of them soon retired to the highest nest, which was now fully exposed to the sun. After throwing out leaves and bark he lay down, his belly full, to dry his fur in the morning sun. The largest of the trio eyed his old nest. He climbed towards it but passed on, climbing higher to swing himself up into another tree. There he started making himself a new nest in a very exposed position, out in the sunlight.

He bent over four large branches sticking out from a fork, broke them inside, sat on them, and packed them down with his fists, slowly turning round in a circle. Then, from his sitting position he reached out to snip off smaller twigs which he put inside also. His companion climbed up to the new nest to inspect, got in and immediately rearranged branches, twisting off some more. The platform took the two heavy bodies easily. It swayed under the blue sky as they worked to make themselves a place in the sun. After some time they sat still and observed the world below; finally lay down. It was now past 8 a.m. and the sun was getting hot.

For another hour everything was quiet. No sound came from the nests, no movement. Undoubtedly they had gone back to sleep, like three lazy bachelors on a beach in deck-chairs after a large breakfast.

Yes, that was what *I* wanted for comfort: a deck-chair !

Sitting on my branch, my legs felt too long, my arms too weak, my clothing sticky. A small squirrel came near to look me over with its beady eyes. A striped lizard ran up and down my branch, hunting for small insects. In spite of these diversions—and for the first time since we had set out into the jungle to see Orangs—I wished I was far away from them. I felt I could not sit any longer; that if my body was untied I would fall down like a ripe durian.

The hour stretched out, minute after minute. Between heaven and hell I felt utterly miserable, out of place. No, the trees meant nothing to me; they gave me a feeling of unreality. Must not Orangs feel like this when they come to the ground, cut off from the lofty height and swaying branches, when forced to walk on feet made for climbing? Bob's bear-like dance seemed in this light an attempt to make the best of an impossible situation rather than an expression of exuberance; his rolling head over heel across the lawn in Pig Lane an only way to gain speed along the ground.

Round about ten the three Orangs became active again. One climbed into a low tree nearby, where a large branch had broken off. He scraped around in a hollow which had filled up with water, bent right down with protruding lips to sip, then put his hand in the puddle and scooped out leaves and water. He inspected his hand and turned it round to suck more moisture from the wet hair on the back of his fingers.

Meanwhile, one of the others had broken off the whole crown of a young tree. Hanging with one arm from a neighbouring branch, he inspected and fed on the young leaves of the crown, then took the tip and carried it into the new nest. There he peeled off the bark with his teeth, chewing some and spitting it out again, until the branch was clear and white. Then he held it over his head for a moment and built it into the nest.

But now his nest companion came towards where I sat. He was sipping dew off orchids and moss growing on a nearby tree. Sheltering my face in the leaves, I felt like a child hiding behind the palm of a hand.

A blast rang out from my right. A series of deep barks and grunts, a scrambling of three red bodies away from the noise of the gun. They disappeared quickly into the trees. I sat in confusion. I had forgotten about Gaun.

It took a long time to get down. I had to get the stiffness from my body before I was able to climb. I sat, rubbing my feet, stretching limbs and body. Gaun helped me pack up the gear.

"Did you *have* to shoot ?"

"I shot in the air because they would have got too near you any minute." Gaun, full of fatherly intentions, untied the rope and let down the equipment.

We were back in camp about noon. It was a sorry return to a shambles of wet beds and blankets. We made a fire and took a sip from the brandy bottle. Bakar returned with the news that our three friends had moved fast and far, without stopping. We decided to call it a day and walk down-river to the next long-house and try another area. At least we had now seen and observed Orang: at sleep, feeding, building nests, wandering. We packed our things and started on the long walk back.

7

An evening in a Dayak long-house is delightful if you come in from the jungle. You relax in a friendly atmosphere, talk, eat, sleep with sympathetic people.

We climbed the notched trunk leading up to the house, built on a forest of poles, about ten feet off the ground. Although Gaun had no friends or relations in this Iban village, it was not difficult to make ourselves at home. We walked over the swaying floor of split bamboo along the dim, long gallery—the *ruai*—towards the middle, where we would find the headman's quarters. Men and women looked up from their work to ask a friendly "wherefrom" and "whereto." A crowd of children followed behind.

The headman's wife, a slender, middle-aged woman with jet-black straight hair tied in a knot, in a black sarong to the waist, came to greet us. A rattan mat was brought by a young girl, spread for us to sit. We offered cigarettes, explained where we had been and what we were doing. Gradually a crowd assembled to hear and see.

"My husband is away in the fields," explained the headman's wife, "he will be back later on."

The house was large, well built with plank walls; the roof, made of palm leaf, was supported by straight, tall rafters of timber. Through small openings along one side where we sat one could look over the open veranda—a wide bamboo platform all along the house, where laundry hung to dry. Along the other, and facing us, was a row of doors leading into the individual family compartments, a fighting cock tied up outside each one—the hall-mark, pride and pet of the head of each family.

"How many doors has your house?" I asked. (In this way you find out the size of a village.)

"Twenty-two—but we want to build some more."

This was about average. It means that along the *ruai*, which is communal, open from front to back with entrance and exit and taking half of the house's floor space, is a series of twenty-two doors which lead into as many family compartments, taking up the other half. Each compartment has a fire-place, one or two small windows and a jumble of family property along the walls: large earthenware storage-jars, suitcases and cupboards, bedding rolled up in mats, often a clock, a sewing-machine, baskets and nets, plates and cups, knives and hats. Each usually houses a big family, of three generations or more, cats and kittens as well.

Heavy farming equipment and an overflow of other things are kept on the *ruai*. Here also, the trophies and sacred objects of the old days hang from the rafters: human skulls, several together in a bundle, bound up in loose rattan baskets, smoked black by fire, covered with dust and spider-webs. Nowadays nobody gives them much attention but they are kept in their proper place because the older generation values them ; they used to be the most important things in a house. They are there to remind the community of the old days of wars and peace-making, of the glory and bravery of their ancestors.

Two young girls came out of the headman's quarters carrying round enamel trays.

"Take something," the headman's wife gave a glass of coffee to each of us, "you must be tired."

Young men crowded round Gaun and Ina, looking with interest at their guns and equipment. Their hair was cropped short, they wore singlets and shorts. Some had tattoos (such as a star, fish-hook or sergeant's stripes) on arms, legs and shoulders; others not. They were the young generation who had done away with the old tradition of long hair, loin-cloth and intricate patterns of spirals all over the body. They had adopted new standards of beauty and smartness. They liked guns and outboard motors, long trousers and shiny shoes (worn on special occasions), gay western shirts or pyjamas, and wrist-watches. They liked education, radio and beer. They lived and worked in the same way as their fathers and grandfathers had done, though with less inhibitions. They were keen on visitors who came from the outside world—for talk, news and fun.

Young women are less eager to adopt new standards. Those living near the coast were the first to imitate any new style. The long hair came off and was curled up in permanent waves in the Chinese manner. Next a bra or blouse was put on to cover the breasts ; not for modesty but for smartness. Simply because town-women—Malay and Chinese—always wore them covered. In a community where women had left their breasts uncovered for centuries, the question whether this may be immodest or not did not arise. They were, or are, naturally exposed, no matter what size or shape. They were worn in the same way as the face is worn and discussed, like eyes, nose and mouth, during adolescence and from a more practical point of view after childbirth. After that any special interest fades. Nobody takes any notice, except perhaps an erring child.

An old woman sat next to me with a small boy of about three in her lap. He suckled one of her breasts and stared at me with big, brown eyes. Grandma caught my smile.

"He is a shy one," she said, "he likes it for comfort—though it is dry—when his mother is away in the fields."

The women who had come to sit near me were still old-fashioned. Only two of the most shapely ones wore bras and lip-stick. Some had children in their laps or at their breasts. They asked lots of questions in their own language. Had I got a husband? Had I children? Father, mother, brothers and sisters? In far-away England? How many years had I lived in the capital? In what kind of house? How much did my golden bracelet cost? My ring? Did I always wear trousers? My hair like that (one long, untidy tress)? Could I allow them to rearrange it? Could I come and see their quarters, now . . . please?

"I must have a bath first." I got up.

"And please," said the headman's wife, "you will sleep and eat with us inside." She took me into her room, helped me with my things.

"Anywhere you like," she said, spreading a new mat on the floor, "we are not many in here."

"You must show me your things later,"—I was eager to see her old jars and gongs, mats, baskets and weavings closely—"but first I must go to the river."

A series of tree-trunks led down the slopes to the water, notched here and there to ease the balance, but without hand-rail. I picked my way, feeling like a fool for my clumsiness as a line of girls queued up behind, soap and toothbrush in hand, to share the bath, some with empty gourds to fetch water.

We swam, sarongs blowing up in gay balloons. Then we sat on the edge, soaping our bodies, washing clothing and slapping it over the tree-trunks. A woman took her small baby and bathed it, holding it softly in the water. Two people from up-river fastened their boat on one of the trunks and carried their things into the house. Small boys and girls were diving in and out, jumping from boats and tree-trunks, chasing each other in the water, screaming, showing off. Wet and refreshed, we returned. It was nearly dark.

The evening meal, a delicious dish of cucumber, onions and pumpkin to go with rice and fish, was taken with the headman, who had returned from his farm-hut in a distant clearing. I asked him about Orang-utan.

"They are never anywhere near our house or fields," he said, "nothing for at least a day's walk in any direction. A few weeks ago when I was on a hunting trip along the swampy forest of the upper Munong stream towards Sebangan I saw some nests, but no Maias."

He explained that his people were well aware of the fact that they must not shoot Orang. They did not dare to go near anyway because people had been assaulted in former years when a good price was paid for them—dead or alive—and some had got wounds, arms or legs bitten right through.

His son-in-law, a young man in his twenties, related a different story. "When I was walking on the old path that was used by the *jelutong* tappers during the Japanese occupation near Sungai Laut not long ago, I noticed remains of Maias' nests, young tops of *Rotan dudok* and the soft bark of the *Empetir* tree which had been eaten that day. I was on my own and walked quietly. When I came to a clearing I saw four Maias sitting in the sun among boulders. They were two adults with two babies who were playing on the ground. They did not notice me. I looked on. I thought it must be nice to catch the babies. I stalked nearer. And then, with tremendous shouting, I bounced into the clearing. You should have seen it," he said laughing. He rolled himself a cigarette.

"The mothers scrambled away a few yards in fright, grunting, but came back for their babies who had started to scream with high-pitched whines. For a moment I had a chance to take them —but I did not dare because of their mothers."

I asked him how old he thought the babies had been. He

A jungle Orang-utan in a durian tree. They hold the spiky fruit in the palm of the hand and bite off the stem

Right, a young Orang on his nest, inspecting a durian. The thick chestnut hair keeps him warm against the rain. *Below*, chewing the durian's large stone

looked down at his small son who played in his lap with an empty tin.

"As big as a child of about two—they were clinging to their mothers to get into the trees, and I found much loose Maias hair in the clearing, as if they came to this place often, to dry their fur."

One of the others said that he also had heard that Maias come down to the forest floor at clearings or to sunny boulders, in order to dry their fur.

"Even old males come to these places. Once somebody told me that a spot near Sungai Sebangan was the regular haunt of an old male. He was so fat that he had extreme difficulty in climbing a tree. He used to sit on a large boulder in the sun, but people were afraid of him. There were always great quantities of hair on the spot."

I asked if they had ever seen male and female mating, or living together and breeding a family.

"We have never seen it," said the headman, "but this would be a hard thing to do. You see many nests from below, but then you don't know if they are occupied. They always keep quiet when they hear people walking on the ground. Mostly there are two or three of them together . . . only old males keep to themselves."

He smiled. "They are different from us in that respect."

It was always the same. We had spent over a fortnight in the jungle with chance meetings here and there and records of nests old and new, two or three younger animals together, and old males living separately. We had not seen an adult female with baby, had had no chance to observe group and family life. To do this, one would have to follow a group for weeks, perhaps months, going after them on the ground while they swung easily from tree to tree into a distance too far; or letting you go by sitting undetected on a high branch or nest and moving away in a different direction once the ground was clear! They were strong, intelligent and independent, with only one serious enemy: the man with a gun.

Gongs sounded from the *ruai*, the call of girls to boys for the fun of the night.

"You should have come after harvest-time," said my hostess, "when we make plenty of rice wine. People get very gay then and keep on all night long. At the moment there is nothing, just a bit of fun."

We took the pressure lamp—a sign of distinction—outside to sit with the crowd. I could not refrain from asking for more Orang stories; and did they think it possible for an Orang to carry away a maiden?

"A relation of mine told me a story like that and it is certainly true. This happened not long ago, during the Japanese occupation."

The headman's wife said that her relation's name was Serai and that she was still living. She had a husband, Suboh, and a son, Bakar. Serai had told it to her like this:

"One morning when I was about to start harvesting, at the time full was the moon, I told my husband Suboh that I had finished making ready the various stuff for the offering—such as *ketupat*, *sungki* and *rendai*. I only had not yet pounded the *tepong*, but I would do it that evening.

"When all was ready on the morrow I went out to start the harvest at our farm on Bukit Lamat. Not long after I had left the house, cock crowings still could be heard (it was so early). Here I saw a *nendak*[1] omen bird hopping cheerfully on the middle of the path. Seeing it, I prayed:

'If you are a bird which brings for me good luck, then you must give me a padi charm, a glutinous padi charm, a tidal stone, a wave stone, a water stone, a rice stone, a stone to be used by me to reap, a stone which can be used by me to take the soul of my padi, a stone which can cause me to become lucky—so that without too much work I can fill my padi bin and easily purchase *sergiu* or *guchi* jars. I want your help.

[1] The White-rumped Shama (*Copsychus malabaricus*), which often comes to the forest floor, is particularly difficult to approach.

I want luck from you, O *nendak* bird. I am now going off to start my harvest.'

"When I finished my prayer, I went straight to the farm. After I had finished with the *matah* (plucking a few first ears of the padi), I strolled about to look for cucumber and its leaves. Then I returned along the same path, home.

"When I reached the spot where I had seen the *nendak* bird, there I was suddenly embraced by a maias, who came from my rear. I fell down to the ground. My basket also was dropped to the ground—and all the cucumbers poured out. These at once attracted the Maias who freed me to pick the cucumbers. These it took up into a tree-top.

"I immediately shouted for help. Many people came—and because of the alarm, somebody beat the alarm gong. The people who came were those from Sg. Tuba, Bt. Plai and the rest as far as Sihut's house at Sg. Pendawan in the Ulu Sebuyau.

"All those who came armed themselves with war weapons such as knives, swords and spears and so on. After they had been told what had happened, all agreed to fell the trees near the one where the Maias was. They felled the trees from morning till dusk; but still the Maias could not be caught.

"That night Suboh slept at the foot of the tree where the Maias was. All the shrubs around it were felled in order that the Maias might not escape. The work of felling trees continued all that night, and at dawn they stopped in order to smoke and have some rest, while one or two guarded the movement of the animal.

"Finally, Sambang anak Dabong started to fell the actual tree in which the Maias was. When the tree came down, the Maias ran off. They speared, cut and did everything else to it, but the animal was invulnerable. It only had some small cuts on its body.

"The Maias now started to climb up another tree. When Suboh realised that it was nearly midday he commanded that a meal be taken. After the meal, Suboh ordered that all the trees near the one which the Maias had climbed now must be felled.

He said that everyone must be careful, for if the Maias could not be killed by them this time, it would be very harmful to them later. 'O, what Suboh said is true,' agreed the others.

"As they felled the tree where the Maias now was, they saw an *azimat*[1] charm stuck to the Maias bundled with a yellow cloth. When the tree was ready to be felled, they chose one Balin anak Salau to bring it down. At about 3 p.m. the tree came down. When it was just about to fall, Suboh saw the animal throw away the *azimat* together with a twig, which he (Suboh) collected. All the remainder of the day they were busy slaying the Maias, which was killed late in the evening. After the death of the Maias, they all returned home. Suboh said that the charm which the Maias threw away could not be found.

"Some time later I (Serai) had a dream of being asked to collect the twig stone around the tree stump. This I handed to my husband Suboh. He lost it some time ago. When it was still in our possession, anyone who used it became very very strong— *gagah* !"[2]

A cock crowed. A cock ? Surely it was too early yet ! But soon it would start, still in full darkness, the inevitable morning concert of cocks—a contest from door to door in the long-house. In the long-house, on the *ruai*, where young bachelors slept—and dogs—it was never really quiet.

[1] A sort of Malay charm to cause one to become very strong indeed, "like Samson of old."

[2] This story was written down by Gaun, and subsequently published in the *Sarawak Museum Journal*, IX, 15, 1960.

III

Educating Orangs

When animals and men meet, it is the
rule that the animal can learn more about
man from his expression than man about
the animal, unless, of course, the man is
using any special equipment. Many animals in fact are equipped with literally
superhuman sense organs and superior
strength and shortness of reaction time.

Prof. Dr. Heini Hediger,
Zürich, 1955

I

THE RETURN TO KUCHING AFTER THREE WEEKS' EXPLORA-
TION in the Sebuyau area was celebrated by way of a hot bath
and luxurious relaxation in comfortable chairs. We had learned
and seen much in the jungle and had followed up every piece of
information. Yet we had made no essentially *new* observation.
Unable to follow any of the animals for long, we had had no
glimpse at mating, at mothers, at social life, organised groups.
The dream of seeing and understanding some of the fundamental
attitudes of one of our closest relations in the evolutionary tree
had become something of a fantasy. The Orangs had been
stronger than we in their own world of trees.

But the trip toughened my approach. I made up my mind to
try and be a true ape-mother from now on. The children would
have to spend much time in the trees instead of on the ground.
Perhaps they could learn to build themselves nests. Anyway,
they should live as free of me as could practically be.

Eve was a big girl now; two and a half and as jealous as
ever. Bill had grown quite fat. He had already developed a
pouch under his chin and Bidai reported that he was very greedy.
Frank was much more slender and lively. All three greeted me
with mild enthusiasm.

A group of fruit trees stood conveniently apart on a slope in
the back of our garden.

"From now on," I said to Bidai, "put them *into* these trees
every afternoon. Don't bring them down, even if they climb
high. Let them do as they please."

He did not like the idea and protested: what were we to do
if they tried to get away? I told him not to worry. We must see
for ourselves, I said.

Eve was fearful at first. Every time Bidai put her in a tree
she came down again to be cuddled. I teased him:

"You have spoilt her too much! Look; she behaves like a tiny baby, she cannot be without you!"

He was indignant. Had he not looked after her well always? Given her food, leaves to play with every day? Cleaned her cage, bathed her, never, ever smacked her?

"She must *learn* to grow up, Bidai, live in her own world, get away from babyhood. Don't allow her to cling to you, teach her to stay in the trees! Sit up there *with* her. Perhaps she will get used to it then!"

So he climbed half-way up the tree, and she went too, first clinging to him and then finding her own way.

It was easier with the babies. Frank behaved as if he had never been away from trees. He climbed swiftly, selecting slender branches and creepers where his small fists and feet could grip and went right to the top. There was no question of fright or even hesitation: he was clearly enjoying himself. Bill followed, but did not go high. Both fed on fruit and leaves and then played, swinging and chasing each other.

When Bidai came down from his perch later, both Eve and Bill followed to romp on the ground near him before he took them to their cages at dusk for their supper of milk, rice and fruit. He asked me what to do about Frank, who was least attached to him and independent by nature.

"He does not want to come down. Shall I go after him?"

"Let me try first," I said. "Perhaps he will make up his mind if I show him his supper."

It was nearly dark and I could see him sitting high up in the tree, a small black shadow. I took his feeding bowl and called:

"Frank . . . Frank! Come down for your supper!"

I sat where he could see me and called again. He squalked once and started moving down. Half-way down he stopped and sat watching me.

"Frank . . . be a good boy . . . come down to your mama!" I lifted his bowl to lure him.

Another squeak and he came, straight into my arms, to be cuddled and have his supper. He ate this greedily, right under the tree. I petted him and took him to his cage to bed. Bidai was impressed.

"I think he would not have come for me," he said. "He likes you better."

He was perhaps right. Frank, though I did not spend much time looking after him and seldom carried him about, seemed to have formed a spontaneous attachment to me. It became a ritual every evening for me to call him down. There was no need to take his feeding bowl. As soon as he saw me he started to come, straight down to the branches immediately over my head. When he was two or three feet above me he let himself fall into my arms.

All young Orang-utans, as long as they are in the baby stage, form an immediate attachment to *any* human being that feeds and looks after them, however poorly. They adopt this person as a mother-substitute, adapting themselves to the conditions imposed on them and making the best of the situation. Depending on the care they will develop certain characteristics : fear and anxieties of a neurotic type if they are treated badly, extreme naughtiness and exuberance if they can do what they please, phlegmatic disinterest and immobility if they are left in a confined space with nothing to arouse their curiosity and emotions. All these conditions can lead to sickness and death in extreme cases.

But apart from this mother-attachment—which any small baby needs to survive—an Orang may express sympathies, antipathies or indifference towards human beings and thus express his own personality in this setting. One outward expression of this is his look. Each Orang has a face of his own, with the eyes as centre of expression. It is impossible to mistake one for the other.

All our children had expressed these sympathies : for Bob it was Tom ; Eve loved Bidai most. Frank was *my* baby although I never encouraged him. Bill seemed to like *himself* best, next to Frank perhaps as a source of entertainment and object of teasing. Yet they had, from the start, all been treated in the same way, like stepchildren of a big family. Eve was spoilt by Tom and myself when she had been a sick baby, much more than Frank or Bob ever had. Yet she treated us with marked unconcern, only caring for Bidai visibly.

These sympathies are often formed at first sight and are more accentuated the older an animal is when faced with a new person— as we shall see. Once at ease, the young Orang will look you over, look *at* you, then take a sniff. At first, by carrying the smell to his nose on his own finger with which he has touched you lightly. Secondly, by bringing his nose down close to your skin on hand or arm. But he *may* even decide to dislike a person *by looks only* —not take the trouble to smell. *If* he likes you, he may tell you so by gesture, by banging and teasing, a grip at your hair, a friendly bite of your finger. And by squeaking—a token of speech. If he dislikes you he treats you with complete disregard, at best.

"I am worried about Eve—and Bidai," Tom once said to me when we were on our evening stroll round house and garden.

"She seems to have got herself into hysterics about him. I think the time has come for Bidai to go on leave—to go back to his village for some time. Ina is well capable of looking after the animals. Eve will just have to find a way for herself to cope with the situation. She must learn to do this or, I am afraid, she will never be anything else than a zoo animal. Let's see if it works."

Bidai went. I think he was glad for a change because he had taken a lot of local teasing lately for his love of Orangs—and for being the object of their love. Eve continued to accept her food as usual and showed no signs of distress.

But she remained reluctant to climb and play freely in trees in the afternoon and dependent on affection and attention to a much higher degree than Bill or Frank. Apparently she was not tough enough by physiology and character to change her ways and adapt herself to a life half-wild. Perhaps it was too late at her stage of development to perform such change; or her experience in infancy (when she was kept under a house on a

94

chain) had for ever destroyed her urge to develop into a free and "wild" personality.

We grew sure that it was better for her to change to zoo-life before she grew older. I made inquiries at Berlin where a new ape-house had just been completed. They accepted the offer, delighted, and presently arrangements were made for her transport by air, from Singapore.

2

Because "everybody knows everybody" in Kuching town, there is—apart from the local paper, the *Tribune*—one source of interesting news which makes the round quickly : gossip passed on with a wide variety of dexterous comments. Though mischievous at times, most people don't take it seriously. It is a good way of entertainment. I know no better cure for my husband's temper when he comes home after a long, hot day, than to pass on some of the trivial things I might have heard in the shops or other places during the day, neatly packaged with speculation. His mind clears : the little world is round.

One day in November, 1958, something wonderful had happened in the gossip world. Nigel Cornwall, the Bishop of Borneo—an imposing man of middle-age—had got engaged. He announced the fact in the *Tribune* ; and that he was going to be married to his fiancee in far-away Ceylon, a few months hence.

On account of this, I was for once eager to get to town early, to talk and listen. But I stopped short when a lorry came up the steep drive to our house with a large wooden crate on top. A forest guard in khaki uniform with green collar got out.

"Here is an Orang-utan for you," he said, smiling. "It was brought down from the Rejang River. Illegally kept by Chinese."

We took the cage down and peeped inside through the wooden bars. The animal looked in good condition. We opened the cage and he looked at us without sign of fear. He had a wire chain round his neck. Gently talking to him, we took it off and

95

he rubbed his neck where it had become sore and hairless. He was a male, the largest ever on arrival—about two years old.

Though he was *not* yet past middle-age, and *not* yet engaged, there was only one name for him : it had to be "Nigel."

Nigel was very independent from the start ; he did not really need us as far as he was concerned. He did not cling for protection and comfort. He took the food offered, both milk and fruit, with complacency. He was not surprised to see his adopted brothers and sister. He was cordial but he kept his distance. We decided that in spite of the chain he must have been kept well, because there was nothing neurotic about him. Or alternatively, that he had a very strong personality of his own, bishop-like . . .

But like all Orangs he had one weakness : Tom. Nigel greeted him for the first time like a friend of old. He came out of his cage, sat down on his haunches and looked. And then his hand came up to pull at Tom's sarong. Tom, holding tight the slipping cloth, played back and grasped Nigel's cheeks and neck ; Nigel opened his mouth wide in a broad grin. It was the beginning of a special friendship.

Nigel's relations with me were different. He treated me with distaste. My diary notes on the 3rd December, *when he had been with us for over a week,* read :

> "When I go to say good-night at his cage, *Nigel for the first time touches me voluntarily.* He does it by poking with his index-finger at places of interest on my arm.
>
> "These are : (a) A broad scar on the skin of my elbow ; (b) my watch-strap ; (c) a ring on my finger.
>
> "He touched each of these—then took the individual smell from his finger by bringing it up to his nostrils."

So far there had been no attempt to tease or play, no squeaks or signs of any recognition. His behaviour towards Bidai was similar. He took Bidai's care without protest, but never showed affection or interest. Only gradually did he learn to accept the routines.

Nigel had arrived at a moment when his integration into our home was possible without much upset. Eve's transport cage had been made during these days. It was important for her to go quickly before a German winter had set in. Bidai took her on the first leg of the journey by sea, soothing and protecting her for the last time.

She reached her new home within six days, and became the youngest, most beautiful and spoilt member of a group of young Orangs in Germany.

Her loss was glossed over by the fact that *three* little faces were now peeping at us, mornings and evenings, through the bathroom door.

We confined Nigel for a few days to the cage to let him get used to his new home. On the 2nd December we took him out into the garden for the first time. He was too frightened even to go into the trees. He played with Bill on the ground, while Frank went up high as usual.

Next day we put up a ladder for him under a fruit tree to give access to the first branches of leaves where it was easy to climb farther. He delighted in the ladder—hung from it, stood on it and pulled down Bill or Frank when they came up on their way into the tree. After some time he went into the tree himself to eat leaves, poke at bark, climb up and down, and generally investigate. He came down within an hour and later followed Bidai of his own accord when he took Bill to the cage for his evening meal. Frank, as usual, had to be called down by me.

On the third day, the 4th December, however, something unexpected happened. Nigel had stayed in the group of trees all afternoon without ever coming down. In the evening he refused to return. Bidai told me that he was unable to catch him, what should he do?

"Leave him," I said, looking out over the veranda, "we shall see what he does—perhaps he has decided to sleep in the trees."

Nigel had managed to get out of the usual group of trees over one high branch that led into another at the very back of the garden. He sat on our very high old durian, about sixty feet up, on a branch with sparse foliage. He climbed, exploring, often looking down. At 6 p.m. he settled in one fork and started bending branches inwards to form a platform—in exactly the same way I had observed it in the jungle. He was building himself a nest !

He worked for twenty minutes, first using all branches in the immediate surroundings of the new platform, then going away four times in search of more material from farther away. After each trip he settled down for a few minutes in the nest, turning round and round as if to try its comfort. After twenty-five minutes, as the sun was going down, he lay down to sleep. We watched for another thirty minutes but there was no movement. Once or twice an elbow appeared to scratch. But as full darkness spread over the garden all was quiet.

The sudden outbreak of nest-building after a reluctant acceptance of trees was unexpected. Yet it was behaviour we found to be typical of Orang-utans ; an example of their strongest capacity—that of adapting themselves to new conditions. Nigel's reorientation to a natural state after prolonged captivity was *not* prompt, because it involved a physical as well as a mental process, fundamental in its consequences, and with no margin for "mistakes."

We had tried to find out how long Nigel had been kept on a chain before he came to us. But as in all such cases, this remained obscure. Because of the penalty involved, it was impossible to get true information. Each person who had handled the animal swore that he was no offender, that he had been keeping the animal only out of kindness. Statements, questions and answers became obscured by the long periods of time that elapse when documents or officials travel along rivers into distant forests or long-houses.

Bidai and Ina took turns to watch Nigel from under the tree before sunrise. This was necessary because he had a good chance to get away from the tree he had selected. We had to lure him back on to the original cluster of trees.

He woke at seven o'clock (5th December), and soon climbed out of his nest. We took Bill and Frank under his tree, where he could see us from above, and gave them their morning milk in the garden. A third dish was left for Nigel—to lure him down. He sat high up for about five minutes contemplating this, then came down to sit on a lower branch, looking at us.

"I can catch him now." Bidai was keen to climb up and get him like a good shepherd; "if I go quickly . . . now . . ."

"No, leave him." I had the distinct feeling that if we made the slightest effort to go *after* Nigel now we would have to do so for ever. If he learned to come down of his own accord for a reward of food and petting, we might have a chance to repeat this way of "catching" him (if it became necessary) in future.

Long after Bill and Frank had finished their morning milk, Nigel decided to come down to the ground. He took his milk greedily and more of it than ever before. I petted him, took him back to the cage with the others. He went to sleep in the cage for a long time that morning. Perhaps he had suffered from nightmares—like a woman camping in the jungle after a long period of sheltered sleep under the roof of a house?

Bidai cut that connecting branch to the trees in the back of the garden. In the afternoon we took all three out, as usual. They fed on leaves, bark and fruit for half an hour, then spent the time in play. At 5.30 p.m. Nigel decided to make himself a nest. He made it fairly low down in a broken fruit tree in the same way as before, twisting and bending over the branches on the chosen spot, holding them underfoot, trampling and padding them down. After two or three minutes, Frank joined him. First he looked on, but then—and as if he had done it many times in his life before—he went to collect some twigs which he put into Nigel's nest, padded them, sat on them. Nigel did not object. He allowed Frank to help. Sometimes they were undoing each other's work, changing branches round the other way; often they sat together in the nest. Bill got bored on his own and came to play on the ground near Bidai.

When it was time for their supper, I called out for Frank and Nigel, showing them their dishes of milk. Frank came at once; Nigel took no notice. He stayed in the tree and started ten minutes later, to make himself yet another nest, much higher up, in a very exposed position. There he went to sleep after thirty minutes' work, scratching and generally fussing. He had decided against cage and company. He was tough.

Nigel's next day (6th December) is taken from my diary:

6.45 a.m. Wakes. Sits up in nest, stretches arms wide, looks down. Climbs out of nest, goes into fruit tree. Bidai and self take Bill and Frank with their morning milk under his tree as the day before. Nigel looks on eight minutes from a high branch, with apparent interest. But decides *against* coming down. He climbs into fruit tree, picks and eats the fruit, spitting out the shells. Defaecates and urinates. Continues feeding slowly for about one hour.

8.00 a.m. Goes back to the high nest where he spent the night, improves it by putting new branches into it, sits down to rest. He climbs into the nest by seizing a large branch with one hand which he had left unbent sticking out. He climbs in, feet first. He sits, looks about (very interested in Bidai, who has climbed a tree nearby to cut down branches to be put into the cage), but does not move. Sometimes he pokes for insects on the branches of his nest—sometimes lies down. He always holds on with one hand to the "handle branch" of his nest.

9.45 a.m. Leaves nest and climbs in fruit and durian trees. Swings, breaking away branches, picks at fruit and bark, but does not systematically feed as in early morning.

10.00 a.m. Inspects lower nest in durian, the one built the day before and left unoccupied during the night. He improves it, working on it for five minutes, often looks down towards house and the cage with Frank and Bill inside. As if he were lonely.

10.30 a.m. Lies down to rest in lower nest, does not move much —dozes, scratches, pokes at leaves and bark—looks down, observing what happens about the house.

11.30 a.m. We feed Bill and Frank. They give their whining cries as they see Bidai approaching the cage with their feeding bowls. Nigel comes out of the nest, as if he meant to come down and join in. We put a third bowl in full view for him to take if he wants to.

He decides against it. He continues watching from a high, exposed branch about 200 yards away until the meal is over, the cage shut. He goes back towards the nest. Apparently he is not hungry.

12.00 a.m. Lies down in lower nest for rest—it is very hot. The higher nest in which he slept overnight is now fully exposed to the sun, the lower nest has some shade from an overhanging branch.

1.00 p.m. Still in nest, but in sitting position. He keeps on peeping towards Bill and Frank—who are restless. They look towards the trees where they see Nigel, swing and bang against the wire, bump to the floor to immediately climb up to the higher shelf to peep back at the trees—as if they longed to be able to join him.

1.20 p.m. Nigel leaves the nest and climbs into fruit tree. Starts feeding on fruit systematically as between 7 and 8 a.m. He climbs high into crown, swings outwards on top of the dense foliage and from sitting position bends the tips of branches inwards towards himself to pluck fruit and young leaves, releasing the branch after picking it empty.

1.30 p.m. Bidai takes Bill and Frank out into the garden. They immediately climb the fruit tree to join in with Nigel. They feed for half an hour on fruit and leaves.

2.00 p.m. Feeding and play combined. Nigel keeps the highest (superior) position in the tree. When Frank gets higher, he chases him—swings and bumps into him, lashes at him with branches or arms—often bringing him down. Apparently Nigel enjoys walking along ("proudly") on all fours on a high, exposed branch, looking down.

3.00 p.m. Frank sits in lower nest, which he is improving. Nigel joins him after ten minutes.

3.20 p.m. Nigel starts building a third nest in medium position. He leaves a "handle branch" which he uses for getting in and out and works for twenty minutes.

Bill does not take an interest in the others. He pokes at loose bark he has found on the rotten tree. He uses the index-finger of his right hand, often brings his face close to peel, chew, test insects.

3.30 p.m. Frank joins Nigel in his new nest. But after one minute they are off, chasing each other, and to swing "daringly," with much speed.

3.35 p.m. Bill comes to the ground to sit with Bidai. Bidai has got a portable radio on the lawn to pass the long watch hours like a modern young man. Bill takes an interest in the noise, but more so in knobs, smell and feel of the machine. Bidai ticks him off, tells him to go back where he belongs. But he prefers to play on the ground.

4.15 p.m. It starts raining. Bidai takes Bill back to the cage and Frank comes down, squeaking and softly whining to shelter in my arms. Nigel takes no notice and remains in the tree. Soon sits down in the low nest where he spent last night, in hunched-up sitting position, exposing his neck and back to the rain.

5.30 p.m. It stops raining and I return Frank into the tree for half an hour before bedtime. They swing and play as before.

6.00 p.m. I call Frank to come down for his supper of milk and leave a jug full for Nigel to take under the tree if he wants it. As we feed Frank and Bill in the cage, Nigel comes down for the first time after thirty hours. He drinks the milk greedily, re-peatedly peeps towards the cage. He does not return to the trees, but comes slowly towards us—once making a bee-line to tear down a branch of hibiscus—as we are ready to close the cage door. Bidai gives him a second dish of milk, which he takes. We open the cage for him and he goes inside. That is where he wants to sleep. He crawls right inside a sack and cuddles against Frank.

It rained all through that night. Maybe Nigel had known it was going to be unpleasant in the trees ?

During the next fortnight, Nigel continued within this general pattern of half-wildness, taking his food in the trees sometimes and sleeping in nests, occasionally coming down for additional food and shelter. He spent six out of fourteen nights in the trees and took an average of two dishes of milk and rice per day (instead of three feeds like Bill and Frank). It seemed to depend on three factors whether he returned to the cage or not : weather con-ditions, the wish for company and (increasingly), the wish for additional food—but in this order of importance.

The months of December and January in Borneo are usually very much influenced by the north-east monsoon winds and heavy rains. When it happened, for instance, that he had to take several heavy downpours during one day in the trees, he preferred to come down for a night in the cage, wrapped tight in a sack. He was very keen on sacks and always crawled com-pletely inside with only his head sticking out. Frank preferred to lie *on* a sack, cuddled against Bill or Nigel, but never crawled into it.

Lack of company tormented Nigel after one lonely night and a full day in the trees. On the night of the 8th December, for instance, he had already settled to sleep in a tree, when he suddenly changed his mind. He came down, slowly first, but when he got to the lawn in front of the house he started running, nearly toppling over, towards the cage. We opened it, offering him milk. He was not hungry. With a squeak of pleasure and "recognition" he went inside, immediately settling down with his companions.

It was unfortunate that the cluster of trees in our garden soon ran out of fruit. It would have been possible to get all three animals slowly used to a life half-wild by feeding them less in the cage, forcing them up to collect their own food in the trees. But living in town, where we had no alternative group of trees in fruit, it became necessary for Nigel to come down more and more often, because he was hungry.

Nigel stimulated both Frank and Bill very strongly with his half-wild attitudes. Frank, who was more independent and tough by character, learned readily and quickly. He started to join in at nest-building on the second day (5th December), of Nigel's activity. Only six days later (11th December) when several nests, four "proper" and three "trial," very scrappy ones, never really *used*, had been made by both Nigel and Frank, Bill did try something on his own. My diary reads:

"11.12.58—a.m. re *Bill*. He plays with a branch supplied in the cage for the first time in a manner 'as if to make a nest.' He twists and breaks it inside to sit on the tangled mass, packing it down with his fists. *Is he learning from Nigel?*"

It seemed as if Bill came down less often now to play on the ground during the hours of exercise. But it was a slow process, because he was by character suited to captivity—a quiet life with a ready supply of good food to be got the easy way. It was food he loved most of all; and we had to watch that he did not get all of it all the time; that he did not get too fat.

3

The urge to wander in the jungle over long distances is stimulated in the first place by the necessity to find the daily supply of food. If a group of Orangs comes into a fruit area sufficiently rich to last for many days, they remain in it until the supply has run out. A second, equally important stimulus is the need to satisfy curiosity, to see and find new things, new varieties of food, different kinds of trees.

As both these conditions could not be met in our garden, our Orangs slowly lost interest in roaming and came down to the ground more often. However, they amused themselves for long hours in discovering "daring" ways of swinging and jumping. They would climb up and come down a tree in certain ways and jump over connecting branches into neighbouring trees with increasing speed. They seemed to delight in competing with each other. They never tried one section of the high durian tree, however, where access was particularly difficult, over one thick stem. Once we forcibly heaved them up.

Nigel continued to climb, carefully embracing the trunk with all fours, slithering along in his usual fashion. Bill gave up after trying the same. He was too clumsy. Frank refused to go on. He sat embracing the fork, whining frantically: it was "unsafe" for *him* and he was frightened.

On the 12th December, ten days after his first outing in the same group of trees, Nigel made his first attempt to get away from it. He chose a large fig-tree which stood 100 yards away near the house at the very edge of a steep slope over Pig Lane, its huge crown spreading over the road, about forty feet below. The tree was unsafe for use by Orangs because falling branches could hit any passer-by—and there was quite a lot of traffic.

During an unguarded moment all three had gone toppling over the lawn with Nigel in the lead to climb this new tree. Nigel immediately made himself a nest, very high up. All three were delighted with the new outlet and very keen to investigate the crown in all its aspects—sending a shower of dead branches, fern, orchids, bark and leaves down into the road. We lured them down in the evening and this time it was more difficult:

"12.12.58. Nigel, Bill and Frank got into fig-tree overhang-

ORANG-UTAN

ing the road. At 6.15 p.m., Bidai and myself go under the
tree to call them. None react. They look at us from very
high up (Nigel and Frank being busy with nest-building,
Bill feeding on leaves) but do not make any move to come
down.

Bidai fetches their food to show it to them under the tree.
Bill, on seeing his dish of milk, comes down quickly. Nigel
and Frank are not interested. When Bidai brings Bill to the
cage, I call again for Frank. He comes slowly, whining, but
remains sitting on top of the first fork, about fifteen feet up,
where climbing is difficult. He remains there, frightened to
come farther—and Bidai swings himself up to get him. We
feed him under the tree—Nigel peeping down from his great
height. Then we take Frank to the cage—leaving a dish of milk
for Nigel under the tree. Round the corner of the house we
observe Nigel, to see what he does. He remains sitting on a
branch, looking down, for about ten minutes, as dusk gathers.
He climbs down to half height, sits again. After another five
minutes he comes down to the ground, takes his milk (Bidai
ready to sprint for him at his first attempt to re-climb the
tree). He sits for two or three minutes, looking towards the
house. Suddenly, with great speed, he comes towards us,
making his way to the cage. His urge to be with companions
was stronger than the interest in the wonderful new tree, once
he had taken his food on the lawn."

By mid-January, 1959, the "Orang trees" in our garden
were a sorry sight. Young twigs and branches were broken,
tangled masses of dry leaves—the remains of nests—stuck here
and there over the crowns. We had to give them a rest or all
would die. The only alternatives were some rambutan trees in
the back of the garden, which had the disadvantage of being
near the road and in full sight of a Chinese neighbour's house.

We were little surprised that the new trees, though they had
only a small supply of ripe rambutan, stimulated a bout of nest-
building. Bill improved especially. This time he took to nest-

building properly, both on his own and co-operating with either Frank or Nigel. Nigel decided to remain in the trees for three nights. On the other evenings he came only very reluctantly, because he was frightened of the road traffic whenever he wanted to come to the ground. He was completely at ease as long as he was high up—even looking with interest at passing cars, bicycles, and at the groups of people that assembled in the road to look up at him and his companions. But as soon as he felt like coming to the ground he became very cautious. He did not let himself down unless the road was completely clear, which sometimes took a long time.

On the 20th January, five days after the introduction to the new group of trees, Bill refused for the first time to come down in the evening. He had made a nest co-operating with Nigel and as dusk gathered he remained in the tree, sharing the nest with him. We did not show food under the tree. Frank came readily when I called him.

Unhappily it rained very hard all through that night. I was worried by the downpour. I took my flashlight, went out to see if there was any need for rescue. But there was no movement in the tree and no reply to my soft call. It was still raining at dawn. I took the morning food to the tree and called. Nigel and Bill peeped over the edge of the nest, but did not move. They did not want to come down! Searching my mind for something that might attract them in this situation, I had an idea. I asked Bidai to go and get their sacks.

We stood under the tree, holding out the sacks for them to see, telling them it was time to get away from the rain.

They came instantly—gingerly though, for they were stiff with cold. They sat down on the lawn, their skin goose-pimpled, shivering and shaking. We wrapped them into the sacks, carried them back to the cage. They spent nearly all morning in sleep. For long periods during that night they must have been awake, stiff and cold.

In the afternoon of the same day, Bill seemed frightened of staying in the trees for long. He came down several times, as if he wanted to make sure that he was not going to be left for another night. He never again spent a night in the trees.

Rain and wind can make a night up a tree rather miserable for an Orang. As long as animals are in the baby stage, up to about eighteen months, they get close protection through the bodies of their mothers. Until he was about twenty months old (20 lb.), Frank came down whenever it started to rain, to cling for protection. Later, like Bill and Nigel, he sat hunched up in the heavy rain, letting the drops run down over neck and back ; usually near the main tree-trunk under a protecting roof of leaves. But as a nest is more exposed to wind and rain, Orangs may get really cold in bad weather. Sub-adults, who have left their mothers, cuddle in pairs to get additional warmth. If they get used to the comfort of a cage for long periods, they prefer to return to it at night, thus increasingly losing the capacity to withstand cold and rain.

The longer our experiment of letting our Orangs live "half-wild" lasted, the more we were convinced that unless we could make it tougher and harder for them to survive, they would become unfit for a life in the jungle. Their ability to become "human" was too remarkable.

4

All through the latter months of 1958 our Orangs remained healthy. There were no colds, bouts of diarrhoea or new worms. We kept a monthly weight-check ; increased their daily dose of milk and fruit slightly if we found that the weights remained constant. But in the first three months of 1959 Frank stopped gaining weight, whereas Nigel and Bill went up steadily. What was wrong ?

Bidai told me that Frank probably did not get his proper share of food. The problem was not apparent when Nigel was living much of the time free in trees. But now that he slowly settled back to cage life, the harmony of our group grew a little disturbed in the confinement of the cage. Frank developed an almost neurotic aggressiveness : he teased the others and constantly felt the need to defend himself as the smallest of them. Because of this attitude, which was emphasised during feeding times when Bill became "greedy," Frank had almost lost the capacity to spread his feed as an Orang should—quietly and slowly, preferably in small bits and pieces all through the day. We spoon-fed him his milk, but apart from that he did not seem to get much.

Outside feeding times he seemed hysterically jealous when Bill and Nigel amused themselves in the cage. It was not *just* a matter of food ; there was a psychological problem too.

We tried the easiest way to remedy the situation : we put Frank in a separate cage during the mornings, next to the others. But he seemed unable to bear it for long, and after about half an hour he always started whining; sometimes he screamed violently. We eased it off by separating him at feeding times only ; and by sometimes placing either Nigel or Bill separately, to give him the feeling that he was treated in the same way as the others. It was not a good solution, however, for it troubled the Orangs.

Another way of solving the problem would have been to build a new, larger cage away from the house, fencing in some of the trees as well. Quite apart from the cost, this idea did not attract us, simply because we would have created a zoo-substitute in this way. And this necessarily led us away from our original aim : to educate them half-wild.

This was the time when we took stock of how far we had got, and what we had been able to achieve. Our original aim, clearly, had been to re-educate our Orangs back towards a life in the jungle, in order that we might rear them up to sufficient size and then let them go again. Nigel's behaviour, and subsequently that of Bill and Frank, showed that it was possible to educate them to climbing in trees, to living in nests and to wild-life feeding attitudes. But there was more to it than that.

Both the comforts and the confinement of our garden at Pig Lane were opposed to carrying the experiment further. What was now required were *less* comforts and a real *territory* sufficiently large to incite roaming; and an adequate food supply within. Unless we were able to fulfil these conditions, our Orangs would now develop away from half-wildness towards domesticity and eventually become zoo animals.

Undoubtedly, during some of the year, wild Orangs are pressed for food, forced to roam considerable distances and, as human population expands and rapidly increases all over Borneo, to come into closer contact and sometimes conflict with man. The better the areas for fruit and other food in Orang terms, the more attractive they are likely to be to the increasingly land-hungry Dayaks. One of the Orang's tragedies is that it is in many ways so closely human; although highly adaptable in diet, just as man is, nothing will compensate for the lack of at least occasional but rewarding periods of heavy eating on readily available rich food, such as the durian.

The next step would have been to start *cutting down* on the diet, simultaneously putting them into a large area of ground within a closely protected sanctuary; thus educating them to roaming. This would require great patience, skill and organisation. It is the sort of thing that would be hopeless if not really well thought out, thoroughly supported from all sides and well financed. It would also probably involve capturing Orangs (for group-contact) and taking other steps which could indirectly do harm in other ways, now that the Orang population is so low and dispersed. The alternative to developing a fully controlled sanctuary for rehabilitated Orangs is, of course, simply to put them back somewhere in the wild.

There are three great difficulties about this. The first and least one is that such Orangs would be dangerously susceptible to easy human approach and simply *asking* to be caught or killed by any comer. So long as Orangs are worth hundreds of pounds, and so long as it is impossible to co-ordinate control between the adjacent territories and along the boundaries concerned, Nigel, Bill and Frank might easily end up, after liberation, in a third-class zoo in Manila or Johore.

The second and much greater difficulty is in seeing that a liberated Orang comes into contact with a group. The existing groups are now so widely scattered and pressurised that they tend to be self-sufficient and/or extremely shy and difficult of approach. A few decades ago it would have been possible to let an Orang go over large parts of Sarawak with the certainty of it being likely to contact others within a matter of days. Now, this is far from being so. Further research is badly needed on the constitution and movements of wild groups.

The third point is that roaming attitudes are developed at an age of about two years, when the Orang is still dependent on *education*. There is a period, roughly between the age of two and four, during which he depends on a certain amount of teaching and incentive to develop proper attitudes which enable him to survive in the jungle. I believe that an orphaned animal must receive this teaching, in an adequate setting, before he is able to live successfully with adolescent companions of his own age—from which stems the foundation of his future adult existence. As during the crucial period he cannot receive this education from man in civilised surroundings like ours he adopts other humanised standards which eventually make him a zoo animal.

The slower an animal develops, the longer is the teaching it requires from its elders. It is quite wrong to assume that a young Orang reacts to a large extent "by instinct." In my view the contrary is the case ; most things are learned through direct teaching, and many fundamental attitudes—climbing trees for instance—are quickly forgotten by babies if they grow up on the ground to the extent of being frightened of any real height.

Babies are taught first and foremost by their mothers, probably for as long as four to five years ; and, from the toddler stage (from about eighteen months old) they also learn from the incentive of their playmates. The Orang's natural curiosity and keen sense to explore, his slow contemplating mind with a capacity to remember events, make him *a priori* highly successful in the jungle. But these very attributes also make him successful, especially as a juvenile, in *human* surroundings, as is the case with our children at Pig Lane. This shows the importance of education. Clearly, to educate Orangs towards successful jungle living, one has to teach it *in the jungle* from when it starts getting away from constant bodily contact with mother.

On the other hand, offsetting these difficulties is one fact of major importance. This is that the Orang has no other enemy but man. Unless it is so foolish as to disturb a hamadryad or molest a nursing honeybear, it is not threatened by any other animal. There is no record, even in semi-fantastic literature of this ape, which reports any other animal successfully attacking an Orang. Therefore, letting an Orang go does not involve the danger common to nearly all other forms of Borneo life—that, fresh to the wild, it will readily fall prey to another species. The only real danger is from man : so if public opinion can be educated and administrative action stimulated and enforced, there seems no reason why Orangs cannot be successfully returned to jungle life.

But apart from such calculation there is feeling, emotion. How can anyone who has loved animals like these bear to put them back behind bars ? That *is* the only alternative, however, unless one is to abandon all other occupation and build one's whole life, home and economy around keeping these animals as they mature slowly to enormous strength. All our feelings are in favour of avoiding sending them into a zoo, even if excellent. This is one of the great heart-breaks in rearing large and slowly maturing animals, rescued from orphanage, damage or starvation.

The dilemma is dreadful. At our worst moments of this kind we would reassure ourselves by pointing out to each other the fate of many Europeans living all around us in Kuching. They have to send their small children off to boarding schools in England, sometimes not seeing them for years at a time. Tom feels very strongly about this himself because he was born in the Argentine and his parents had to live there until he was sixteen. His excuse for some of his aggressiveness is always that he spent years without parental love at horrible schools in term-time and with people who did not really want him in the holidays. He might as well, he says, have sweated it out in a zoo !

Miserably, we eventually decided to solve our Orang problem at home by again giving one of them away. If there was no other alternative, it was better to do it soon, when the animal was still highly adaptable to new surroundings and a change of climate.

Bill was the one best suited to go into captivity. He had been self-satisfied, of balanced temperament, from the very beginning. His response to half-wildness had been slow and rudimentary, he seemed to prefer an easy cage-life with plenty of food. By the end of March, 1959, when spring had come to Europe, we finalised all arrangements with Antwerp Zoo. Bill flew to Belgium, like Bob and Eve had gone before him to San Diego and Berlin.

I wrote to Dr. van den Bergh, Director of Antwerp Zoo, on the 4th April :

". . . make sure that nothing goes wrong at the last stage of the journey. One point is important : Bill is used to much freedom and dislikes being confined in a small cage. I will do what I can from here to build his transport cage as securely as possible and will warn the Singapore people to check the cage before he goes on the flight to London—but Bill is ingenious in finding ways and means to dismantle a cage and he has many lonely hours at hand to work on it . . . Bill weighs now 29 lb. and is in very good health."

He arrived safely and in perfect condition after ten days' journey via Singapore and London ; and without dismantling his cage sufficiently to be able to get out !

5

Six months of uninterrupted cage-tree routine followed for Nigel and Frank, four of which we ourselves spent away from Kuching, excavating in the Caves of Niah, over 300 miles to the north-east. We were often reminded of our children because in all levels of the excavations, even down to the early Stone Age, round about 40,000 years ago, Orang bones and teeth—some of them very large—kept on turning up. They must have been plentiful at that time. Yet to-day, not one lives within 200 miles.

Even in one of the last refuges left in Sarawak they have been lately disturbed by the construction of a trunk road to connect Kuching with Simanggang. The road was taking shape in 1959, through the Balai Ringin and Sabal Forest Reserves, running close to the Indonesian border. Noisy men and machines were cutting a straight line through the dense forest, to take the new road. Once or twice we heard from road engineers that Orangs had been seen.

But it was not until the 28th November, 1959, that we had evidence : a new baby arrived from Balai Ringin Forest Reserve.

This time it was brought directly to the Museum by a Chinese who made a living in the timber business. He came with a basket slung over his shoulder. Inside the basket was the smallest Orang I had ever seen—a male baby, a beautiful little thing—and with it, a milk bottle. We questioned the man closely, and out came one of those stories that may or may not be believed ; he said :

"It was not *me*, mind you, but a friend of mine, several friends of mine, who were hunting in the forest. . . ." He settled for a long tale while the new baby clung to me.

"They were hunting for pig that day . . . there is quite a lot of pig in the area. They were right on the tracks and very close to the pig when one of the men saw it and shot. . . . And suddenly, as the sound of the gun blasted away, there was a great commotion in the trees overhead. A baby Maias dropped to the ground, right to the feet of the hunters, like a durian ! " Then he explained:

"His mother got a shock from the gun and dropped it to the ground . . . but she did not care to come and get it, she made off with great speed into the distance."

He concluded his story, self-satisfied :

"So the hunters had to take the baby, and they have been looking after it quite well ! "

"You have been feeding on milk *only* ? " I dreaded to hear differently. But fortunately somebody had had sense !

"Yes, and he takes a lot—say these friends of mine. They actually want to claim expenses for its food ! And I also want to claim for the time and expense on the bus to Kuching . . . it is only for the baby Maias that I came along ! "

He could not tell me exactly how long the baby had been in captivity. About three weeks, he said. Yet the poor little thing could not be older than approximately four months : it did not have a single tooth !

It was not our concern to deal with the legal aspects of the case—that would be done by the Forest Department. But we wanted as much information as possible, no constructed evidence. So I probed deeper.

"Are you sure the mother dropped its baby just like that ? Don't you think that she was perhaps injured by the shot of the gun ? " But he insisted :

"I am quite certain, because the shot killed the pig ! How can it injure a Maias at the same time ? My friends *know* that they must not shoot Maias, they are afraid of them anyway." And he went on to tell that they had not been aware of the Orangs' presence, did not know whether there had been one or two, or even more—the only thing they knew was that the baby had dropped to the ground !

My first reaction was that of complete disbelief. How could an Orang mother drop her baby—surely a tiny one like that would cling fast to her fur and never leave her for a moment. It was much more likely that they had shot the mother, either accidentally or deliberately, and were now stranded with the baby —trying to make the best of a tricky situation.

Much later, when I had seen an Orang mother holding her month-old baby in her arms—in Frankfurt Zoo during the summer of 1960—doubts came to my mind. The baby was *not* just clinging to her; the mother was *holding* it, supporting its body and drooping head with arms and hand. She took great care with it, quite unlike most monkey mothers, shifting its position with every movement.

It was possible that a mother, if she was suddenly disturbed with the blast of a gun in the immediate vicinity, might drop her baby when her impulse to get away quickly at all costs was too strong for her movements to be careful. A sudden jerking, a swaying branch hitting the baby, might have sent it to the ground.

Since this was written, my husband, while making inquiries about the status of Orang-utans in North Borneo, has come upon a well-authenticated case up there. During November, 1960, a geological party, under Dr. P. Collenette, were surveying far up the Kinabatangan River. A sub-party, led by Stephen Seping, operating near Malog, shot a pig on an evening in primary virgin jungle country, part of the vast uninhabited area there. To their amazement, a large female Orang crashed off in the trees, and a baby tumbled to the ground. This baby was evidently "less than a month old," and though they were trying to keep it alive it died within two days. Until then they had been unaware of any Orangs in the area.

However, to return to "Ossy"—for this was the name I gave our new baby Orang—I went out to buy him a basket for his nest, a cushion and blanket for the night, a baby bottle and special baby milk. Then I took him home in the car. Ossy clung to me all that time, never making a sound, just looking up at my face. I put him on a scale: 5 lb. 12 oz.

At the age of 2½ Eve still clung to Bidai, whom she adored

Frank, Nigel and Bill (Frank at the top) on their afternoon's outing in the trees

I hung his new basket on ropes from the ceiling of the room next to our bedroom, where I could see him at all times ; suspended another pair of ropes to hang over the basket for him to grip and play with ; stuck small branches and flowers all round the wickerwork to look at and chew, if desired. At noon I gave him a bottle of baby milk—the exact amount prescribed for infants four months old. He took it greedily in one go, pushed away the bottle when it was nearly empty, burped, and went off to sleep in my arms before I even put him into his basket. Gently I took his feet and fists from my body, placed him in his basket and gave him the ropes to grip. He did not protest. He peeped over the rim of the basket, played with the leaves, chewed one of the flowers. He dropped off to sleep again like a very good boy.

Ossy, unlike Nigel exactly a year ago, had come at a very inconvenient moment. Tom was away far inland, in the Kelabit mountains, and he was not due back for some weeks. This meant that I was more or less stuck in the Museum—and we were working on new exhibits of archæological findings from the Niah Caves. It was impossible for me to stay at home and look after Ossy. I could not leave him with Bidai either, for he was busy with the others and many other animals and birds we have around the place. It was obvious that Ossy needed a woman at that stage. He wanted a foster-mother for six months at least, who would treat him like her own baby.

I went to see Osie Merry in the afternoon. He lifted both hands in surprise as I stepped into his office with the new baby in my arms ; wrapped in a nappy so that it might not misbehave.

"My God ! . . . I did not realise you would go *that* far ! How on earth did you get this little mouse ? "

I told him the story and he looked him over.

"He seems quite healthy—and not underfed." His initial verdict was promising, but he still wanted to check on his blood and fæces.

"I don't know what to do, Osie . . . he really needs a mother and I have not got the time to look after him properly at present. And unless we do that he will not live ; he is much too small to be able to develop on his own." I explained the situation to him and he thought for a moment.

"I think there is a way . . . Joan might want to take him over for a few weeks until we go on leave." He got her on the phone.

"Joan . . . I have got a baby here in my office . . . No ! Not mine ! . . . a small Orang-utan ! Would you be prepared to look after him for some weeks until we go on leave ? Barbara can't manage at the moment and he needs a mother ! "

When Osie told me that his wife was keen to help I was sorry to have to give him away. But I knew it was best for him ; he would even be under constant medical supervision.

"What is his name ?"

I made up my mind on the spur of the moment.

"Ossy," I said, "for Osie Merry, if you don't mind !" Somewhat lamely I explained to him that all our animals derived their names from benefactors to the cause of Orangs or other figures of grace (cf. Nigel). "You are long overdue, there is no other way. . . . It will have to be Ossy !"

I took him with all his gear—basket, blanket, some quickly bought nappies, bottle and baby milk to Joan. She and her pretty daughter Janie, just turned seven, were delighted.

"Mamie, may I hold him, please! "

"Yes, but careful, darling, he is just like a tiny baby !"

"Mamie, we can give him my old cot—I think he would like that to play inside—and a doll—and . . ."

"Yes, darling, but look—just now he wants to go to sleep, can you see his eyes drop ?"

It was true. Ossy had gone to sleep in Janie's arms. It seemed that he had adopted her within a few minutes, and she him.

I discussed all details with Joan, told her what, in my view, was important for the baby :

To be off the ground.

To be able to grip and hold fast to ropes and branches, so to exercise his limbs.

To have a constant fresh supply of leaves, suspended swaying over his head, to chew and play with.

To be out-of-doors.

To be out of the sun and out of the rain most of the day.

To have a blanket at night.

To be cuddled (but not too much !).

To have no strangers—and above all no one with a trace of cold or lung troubles—breathing over it.

To have a regular routine of feeding times, bath and sleep.

"I don't think he wants any other food than milk yet, perhaps with a regular dose of vitamins," I added. Joan smiled.

"Did you hear this, Janie ? He must have vitamins—just like you, and you never want them ! I think from now on you will take them *together* !"

Janie never again refused her vitamin pills. She took them with gusto, same as Ossy. He fed on baby milk, four times a day, and slept all night from dusk to dawn in his basket, inside Janie's old cot. Joan kept a regular check on weights and within a fortnight his first two teeth, the two lower incisors, cut through. There was great hope that he would live and be healthy.

6

By mid-December, 1959, when Ossy had been with the Merrys for over a fortnight, another baby was brought in from the end of the new road. We heard of it a day beforehand, through one of the road engineers.

He told us that one of his Malay mandors had been asked to look for a baby gibbon which somebody wanted to keep as a pet. The mandor went to see Dayak friends in a long-house not far off. They showed him a baby ape which was kept in the long-house and he paid fifteen Straits dollars for it (£2 sterling). Their story was that it had fallen from a tree they were felling. When the mandor got home, he realised that he had not bought a gibbon, but a baby Orang-utan ! Uncertain what to do, he had kept the baby for three weeks, and was very fond of it.

But the story got round and the senior engineer, aware of the regulations, told him to give it up. He would send it down to Kuching next day.

For the first time I was actually eager to get a baby, because, I thought, if it was anywhere near Ossy's age, it was a fortunate thing to get it. It is so much better for young Orangs to grow up with a companion. They become more independent, get more fun. A companion—whether male or female—fills the gap that always remains between man and ape, however fond they may be of each other !

The baby came. It was a female of just over 5 lb. But she already had ten teeth, which meant that she was approximately four months older than Ossy though considerably under-weight. She had been fed on bananas only ; no milk. She had a broken arm also and, as Osie found out a few days later, was infected with hook-worms. I took her to the General Hospital to have her arm set in plaster, went to town for another set of equipment : basket, bottle, baby food, blanket, nappies and all the rest of it. I took her to Joan Merry, her arm dangling from a white sling in front of her skinny body. Joan agreed with me that it would be very difficult to keep her alive, but she would certainly try and nurse her back to health. We called her "Janie."

Janie settled down in her new home, accepted her first bottle of milk after twenty-four hours. She slowly gained weight. She was not as lively as Ossy, who had already started to pull himself upright against the wooden bars of his cot, slowly working round and round it, but then she was much impaired by the weight of her stiff arm ; and the worm-cure had taken some of her strength as well. After a week of steady progress, Joan was hopeful. And as I went away for some days to accompany my husband, who now had work to do in the Sarawak River Delta, we were already making plans for Ossy and Janie to grow up together.

When I rang up three days later to find out from Joan how things were going (I had got worried) she said :

"It is as if you had sensed it . . . she suddenly died ; yes, this morning."

She later told me that she was very surprised by her sudden

death. There had been no outward sign of deterioration. She had taken her milk, had steadily increased her weight. Round about ten one morning, Joan had looked out from a window into the garden where the cot stood, with the babies inside. They were both resting—as they used to do often in between periods of activity. Nothing seemed wrong, they had quietly been playing with their hands and toes. Ten minutes later she was passing the cot and realised that something was badly wrong. She found Janie dead—with no outward sign of injury. She had gone out like a light, within a few minutes.

Osie checked over her dead body immediately. There was no sign of illness. Theoretically she should have lived, especially after improving so well from the weak state in which she came to us. Perhaps the change of diet had been too abrupt. But I had the strong feeling that, as in the case of the male baby Tony, that had died the previous year, it was also an inability to *cope* with life and its imposed surroundings, a loss of drive for development, which followed on extreme physical neglect and a number of psychological shocks. It is hard to become aware of such a situation in a baby ape, because there are no tell-tale signs for it. But it seems that once a certain border of wild living and loving is crossed, death must be the sudden consequence.

Janie's death warned us how careful we had to be with Ossy. So far he had increased his weight steadily. We noted days and sequence of appearance of his milk teeth. I wrote for information on the few baby Orangs born in zoos, to see how Ossy's development compared. His weight increase was right. The sequence of appearance of his milk teeth[1]—spread from the end of the fifth month to the thirteenth month of his life—were not exactly the same as those published for a male baby raised in Dresden Zoo, Germany, but agreed with slight variations. The first teeth—in every case the two lower incisors—had come on with the Dresden baby on the 151st day, and with another born

[1] See Appendix I, p. 210, for table showing sequence of appearance of milk teeth and permanent teeth, with comparisons of human dentition.

in Nürnberg Zoo on the 139th day. This gave a fairly accurate estimate for Ossy's age when he started teething, of five months.

Setting Janie's weight curve[1] against the weight of the other babies when they had ten teeth, showed that she had been well over five pounds under-weight, thus only about half of what she should have been. This is beyond the endurance of a *human* baby, also.

The physical development of baby Orangs during their first year of life compares intimately with that of a human baby. The birth weight is doubled by the end of the fifth month, treble by the end of the twelfth month. The appearance of milk teeth, though slightly delayed, is similar as in human babies. The Orang baby is just as helpless and dependent on his mother's protection as the human baby. On her milk (or substitute) for food, on her body for warmth. The Orang baby's reactions— screaming for food and whining in case of discomfort, affection towards mother, slow orientation of vision and movement—are the same as those of a human baby. The only fundamental difference is the ability and need to grip, both with fists and feet, to the mother's body and hair. The baby becomes helpless without its mother also, because his limbs have lost their natural hold. It is essential to provide a substitute to hold on to, because it is through all four limbs that an incentive is given to move and climb, to learn and develop.

When Ossy came to us he used to grip with his feet round his own wrists because there was nothing else to hold on to. When he was given ropes and branches as well as the side bars of his cot, he gradually lost that painful attitude.

Ossy was able to walk round his cot at the age of five months, pulling his small body up on the wooden bars. He could also hang free, either from one or from both hands, on a rope suspended overhead. Best of all, of course, he liked to be taken up and "cling to mother"—as long as "mother" was a person he intimately knew. He loved to be with Joan and little Janie, but

[1] See Appendix II, p. 212, for table of weight increase of baby Orang-utans in relation to the appearance of teeth.

not so with me as an occasional visitor. It was therefore with some fear that I took him over from Joan. It meant another change of surroundings and loss of physical "attachment" as well.

When I came one afternoon to load up his cot and equipment, it was a sad good-bye.

"I have sent Janie out to play with other children because it will be very difficult for her to miss him," Joan said. She handed me the baby, wrapped in nappies.

"She would have cried . . ." she added, and I was not quite certain whether Joan herself was not in tears. "I hope he will take on with you. Let me know how it is going to-morrow. If he is very upset it might help for us to come round and see him for a bit. . . ."

I understood how she felt. But we need not have worried. Ossy completely adopted me as his new mother within twenty-four hours. And I told Joan over the telephone that, in my view, it was much better for her to stay away. I felt that a clean break helped him to accept the change better. He was faced with the need to form a new attachment—which he quickly did in order to survive. I knew that one day I would have to hand him over in just the same way.

But not quite yet . . .

7

Ossy continued his fixed routine with four bottle feeds and periods of exercise and rest. His cot—his home—stood in the garden during the day-time, but we placed it inside the house, into our spare bathroom, at night, where he had complete protection from weather and insects. A round basket—his nest—was hung up inside the cot and this he used for sleep. I usually found him still curled up in it at 6.30 a.m. He always crawled out to be taken up as soon as he saw me coming.

He was very eager to get hold of his early bottle, gripped it with both hands to force the sucker into his mouth. He never liked it hot, simply pushed it away again if it was more than hand-warm. He drank six to seven ounces at a time, mostly in one gulp without stopping for breath. When he finished, he released the bottle and shoved it out of the way with the back of his hand. Sometimes—often these were days when new teeth cut through—he took less than his normal due. Then it was hopeless to try and incite him to take more : he spat and coughed, edging away from me. Once he had taken his huge gulp, he had finished, and that was the absolute end of the affair.

Ossy was allowed half an hour of cuddling after receiving each bottle. Up to the age of six months he spent this time, resting or half-asleep, on my lap. Later he was more active and started exploring. At first it was my hair, face and eyes for which he showed interest and affection. Most strikingly, by exposing gums and teeth in a broad smile, sometimes "biting" my nose with mouth wide open, or "combing" my hair with his fingertips. His little face—the triangle between eyes, nose and upper lip— was sensitive and he always turned it away, wincing and blinking, at first contact with strangers. When he was older he started climbing about my chair and around the table, always careful, though, to remain directly in contact, by one hand or foot, with my body.

I liked to take my own breakfast with him still about. He showed much interest in my food and liked to try little bits of everything. He took small pieces of fruit from my lips and ate them ; but everything else, a sip of tea, a piece of bread and butter, wanted to be tested also. If it was no good, he spat it out neatly.

That an Orang baby is introduced to masticated food by its mother at a very early stage is indicated in a report by Dr. Aulmann for Düsseldorf Zoo, where a mother had given birth to a female infant in 1931. The mother "started feeding the baby with her own food (consisting of potatoes and carrots), thoroughly masticated, by pressing her lips against the baby's mouth when it was only twenty-three days old."

EDUCATING ORANGS

But perhaps, in this case, mother herself was inexperienced, because the report continues : "She had done too much of a good thing, apparently. The baby started coughing, spitting and regurgitated its food, whereupon she solemnly fished it all out of her baby's mouth using her tongue. Even on the first day after birth she had tried to arouse the baby's interest by holding a banana in front of his face, but naturally the baby had taken no notice at all. . . ."

It was during these wonderfully relaxed morning sessions with Ossy in my lap, that I sometimes read a newspaper or magazine on the side as well. Soon it became apparent that Ossy not only loved the paper to play with and make a mess of it, but that he was able to recognise pictures, also. Pictures of human *faces* particularly, even if small, incited him to imprint a firm "kiss" on the face's eyes, nose and lip area. It did not matter to him whether they were upside down or the right way up. Later I experimented with other subjects. He showed keen interest in pictures of leaves and flowers which he poked with his index-finger and even tried to chew. The same he did if I wore a skirt or blouse with a pattern of flowers and leaves.[1]

When Ossy's cot had been washed down in the morning it was placed outside, together with Nigel's and Frank's cage, and decorated with new branches and flowers. He started to play

[1] It was not only Ossy who was able to recognise pictures and caressed those of human faces (preferably "cover-girls") in that way. All other babies did the same, though with varying degrees of intensity.

Dr. Hediger, in *Studies of the Psychology and Behaviour of Animals in Zoos and Circuses* (London, 1955), describes a baby female Chimpanzee, Viki, who was able to recognise pictures also. "In Viki's case, this recognition of pictures was most carefully tested, incidentally with her gift for imitating. Her foster-parents taught her to mimic all sorts of actions at the command 'Do this' "—a thing I have deliberately never attempted with my babies. I tried to educate my Orangs in a way which I thought their mothers might have done, in the wild.

with them immediately I put him in, and in this way separation from me was made easy. As long as his interest was aroused by something new, he did not mind being put back into his cot. He liked flowers especially. He picked them off first thing with his fingers and placed them in his mouth to chew off the sweetness. But as the morning wore on I had to be careful not to be seen by him, going in and out of the house too often. For he was easily bored and once he had explored all the things in his cot he wanted to be taken up. His form of request to get out was a loud scream, as soon as he saw me in the distance.

After a mid-morning nap and a bottle at noon, I used to take him into the garden for a bit of exercise. He was not yet able to walk, but he could climb about in low bushes and delighted in this, once he got over the first shock of being separated physically. His arms were now strong enough to hold his body ; and as long as he could see me near, he was quite happy to climb and explore on his own, gradually extending the distance into which he dared to venture.

The report from Düsseldorf Zoo similarly refers to efforts by the Orang mother to educate her baby towards climbing, and it may be concluded that the same sort of thing happens in the jungle also.

"At the age of three months the baby does not move at all yet on his own, although the mother has started educating it towards climbing from its tenth day. She does this by taking the baby with one hand round the waist, and with the other places its hands and feet round the bars of the cage. So far, the baby is very clumsy and does not grip well round anything except the fur of its mother. . . . She also tries in another way to incite the baby to move on its own. She places it, belly down, on the floor of the cage. Then, settling herself on a high shelf, she observes with great interest the baby's efforts to walk towards her—whining miserably while it does so. If the baby makes no progress, she comes down and gives it her finger to grip. Then she pulls it gently along the floor."[1]

Similar observations were made by Professor Brandes at Dresden Zoo. The mother started feeding her baby with masticated food at the age of two months and, when it was three and a half months old, "exposed" it on the floor of the cage. At that age the baby was able to hang freely from both arms, but his lower limbs were still undeveloped and very weak.

Education in cleanliness is another matter. It is probably impossible to teach an Orang that certain spaces should be used for certain purposes, because the animal's instincts are adapted to living in trees where everything drops down, out of sight and smell. But they have a distinct tendency to keep their bodies and nests clean.

Ossy never fouled his nest—the little round basket in which he curled up for sleep. Urination and defecation was stimulated at once when he was taken outside his cot and placed into low bushes or trees for exercise. If he felt a need while clinging to my body he lifted his bottom away from me. But apart from this natural attitude of babies, mothers seem to watch and teach in this respect also :

"Another peculiar exercise the meaning of which was obscure at first, took place several times during the day. At certain intervals the mother loosened the baby's grip, took it with one hand at either arm or leg and let the baby swing freely in the air while she moved about the cage. The baby dangled, screaming wildly . . . and eventually it was observed that after such exercise, and often during it, the baby defecated as a result of the combined shaking and screaming."[2]

The same German mother kept her baby clean—using either water or her own urine—to wash its fur where necessary. I treated

[1] G. Aulmann, "Geglückte Nachzucht eines Orang-utan im Düsseldorfer Zoo," *Der Zoologische Garten*, v 4-6, 1932.

[2] G. Aulmann, ibid.

Ossy similarly, using lukewarm water, but often gave him a full bath when the weather was warm and dry. He liked this very much, as also having his long, shiny hair combed. Another way of grooming was observed in Dresden Zoo. Here the mother, apart from keeping her baby's fur clean and "combed," also neatly bit off its finger- and toe-nails when they grew too long. The baby was then two months old and clinging to its mother the whole time. Later, when the baby started climbing on its own, thereby sharpening its nails on branches, this became unnecessary.

During the early months of life, baby Orangs sleep regularly during day-time. Ossy used to have naps of about thirty minutes after two hours of activity. He lay down to sleep in his basket, sometimes on my lap or, especially if it was hot, simply on the wire floor of his cot. He lay on either side or back, hands and feet gripping the edge of his basket, a rope, or a wooden bar of his cot. His night sleep was uninterrupted from dusk to dawn and only once—on a warm night in April when he was eight months old when something quite extraordinary happened—did he leave his cot during the night.

Quite by accident I woke at about three o'clock that morning, feeling thirsty. I got up to get myself a drink from the fridge. As I put on the light, Ossy's low whine came from outside the front door. Still half-asleep I opened it and found him sitting in the concrete passage which leads to the house, miserably shaking with cold. I took him up, cuddled him ; what on earth had he got out for? I wondered, taking him back to his cot in the bathroom—(this was the second bathroom, at the back of the study, with a door and steps leading outside to the front of the house ; he had got out that way). Here my eyes popped : an army of termites was in the course of invading our house ! They had taken their way up the bathroom steps. They were marching in a broad stream right through Ossy's cot, up the walls and into the rafters overhead.

Immediate action was necessary for they would have disappeared into the woodwork or rafters by daylight. I interrupted the stream by spraying it with an excessive dose of DDT powder, still holding Ossy in my arms. Within half an hour the whole room was a cemetery of termites; but poor Ossy had nowhere to sleep!

Luckily I did not have to deal with Tom, who was away from Kuching! I took Ossy into my own bed. He nestled against the small of my back and went to sleep within a few minutes. He did not hold on to my body nor did he stir until 6.30 a.m. when I took him up for his first bottle.

8

While Ossy slowly developed out of babyhood, Nigel and Frank continued their "half-wild" existence. The urge to build nests at dusk was weak now. They came back every evening, often before it was time for supper. They needed a new outlet, but our trees were exhausted. Across Pig Lane, the Chief Secretary's big garden sloped up to the crest of a hill, with his fine house on top. I coveted the trees of this hill-side for some weeks before I dared ask. Finally, I plucked up courage to do so when in a party mood, and Derek Jakeway was most sympathetic.

"Of course you may let them into my garden if you think they will like it. I'll be flattered!"

We took them across every day. But what we hoped for did not happen. They seldom built nests and never slept in the trees. It was unfortunate that none of the trees were in fruit. Because there was no fruit in any of the trees, there was no incentive for them to fend for themselves. They came back down to the cage for food and shelter each dusk. We put them out in every weather to keep them tough. Bidai stayed with them to watch; if it started raining he sat under an umbrella. One afternoon in February I went to fetch them home early, because the rain had developed into a thunderstorm. When I came up to the trees I could not see Bidai and my call was lost in the up-roar of rain and thunder. I looked up. He sat in a tree half-way up, perched on a branch under an open umbrella. Cuddled on either side were Nigel and Frank sheltering with him, perfectly still and happy. The ground under the trees was a sea of mud. They did not see me until I was right under them. Only reluctantly did they come down to cross through the curtain of rain and get into the car.

Nigel and Frank simply loved to drive in our car. As they had got much heavier and the way to the other garden was steeply uphill, I arranged with Bidai that he walked the boys there after lunch and I came to fetch him by car at tea-time or later. Nigel and Frank knew that as soon as the car came up the steep drive, they were to be treated to a ride home. They came down as they spotted the car, raced towards it over the last bit of lawn, head over heels. Nigel preferred to share the back seat with Bidai, to sit back against the upholstery and look out of the window. Frank took the front seat with me but was too excited to sit down. He stood on the seat, holding on to the window, often sticking his arm or face out to catch the breeze. Or he tried to help me drive by pulling on the wheel or the gear-lever !

By February, 1960, Nigel was weighing 55 lb. and we estimated his age to be three and a half years ; Frank weighed 36 lb. at approximately two and a half years.[1] Nigel was extremely strong and it became increasingly difficult to handle him on Bidai's days off. One Sunday Frank and Nigel made a complete fool of me in our garden. The trees they knew so well did not attract them for more than half an hour. They teased me by constantly "running away" into other sections of the garden where they broke every young tree in sight, unripe bananas, papayas and pineapples. When I ticked them off they thought it was a wonderful game.

Also, their cage, the bathroom "annex," was getting too small for them. Nearly every day they found a new point of weakness and took it to pieces. In fairness to them we had to decide soon on what should become of them. They had slowly graduated to

[1]See Appendix III, p. 213, for the weight curves of Nigel, Frank and Bill.

live in human company and there was no alternative to intro-
ducing them into a very good zoo. Another factor forced us
to decide on their fate soon : we were due to go on leave to
Europe by early May and had a good chance to take them by
sea, looking after them on the way.

Wherever they went they would have to stay together. Because
if they were separated—if only for a visit to Osie or a weight
check—the one left in the cage started to whine most pitifully.
They were used to each other and they needed each other's
company to enjoy life.

Of all the Orang applications we had on file from zoos, one
from Hamburg sounded particularly attractive. There was a new
ape-house where a group of Orangs was kept, including two
females of Nigel's and Frank's age ! We wrote offering to present
them on condition that their fares were paid and that we were
informed of their progress at reasonable intervals.

We had also had a letter from the Zoological Society of Scot-
land, at Edinburgh Zoo. Here a famous male Sumatran Orang,
Mickey, had died of old age after a period of twenty-two years
in the Park. The Director, Dr. G. D. Fisher, wrote :

"Mickey's passing has left us without an Orang-utan in our
collection, and I am sure you will be glad to know that my
Council decided we must not put out inquiries through the
normal channels as we feel that Orangs are still being supplied
by indiscriminate killing of mothers. As a Zoological Society
we are very anxious to do nothing that might encourage such
destruction. It was felt, however, that from time to time
young Orangs might be confiscated from natives trapping on
behalf of unscrupulous dealers and if it were possible to procure a specimen, or better still a pair, in this way, my Society
would naturally like to have the Orang-utan represented. . . .
I trust you will forgive my approaching you with this request
for help as it is chiefly due to the fact that, while strongly
desiring to obtain another Orang-utan, I am anxious that it
should be done only through proper channels. . . ."

For the first time a zoo had expressed concern about the plight of Orangs and decided on a deliberate policy to actively assist conservation. Here, at least, was one ray of hope, even though there may not be a new ape-house.

We wrote offering Ossy. He was too small to be left behind, when we went on leave. We said that he would need very special care until he grew out of babyhood.

Dr. Fisher suggested:

". . . our Overseer's wife, Mrs. Macpherson, would be the best person to look after Ossy, but I don't think he should be kept in the room of a private house. My thoughts at the moment therefore run along the idea of preparing a special little house for him complete with a glass sun-porch, where the air could be conditioned . . ."

By April it was all agreed. I started to make arrangements for the long sea trip. The main difficulty was to find a boat with a captain who was prepared to take my charges and myself as a passenger as well. Passenger boats do not carry live animals as a rule, and it was up to the captain of a cargo ship to decide if he would take live animals. We had refusals to start with:

YOURTEL THIRD OWNERS CONSULTED—REGRET CAN-NOT ACCEPT APES—PATERSIMCO

MRS. HARRISSON YOURS 2ND—REGRET ACCOMMODA-TION FULLY BOOKED AND UNABLE ACCEPT ANIMALS—BENSTEAMER

and so on . . .

As I was fighting the telegraphic battle for the accommodation of three apes, a fourth one came into our home, as suddenly and unexpectedly as the others had. He was announced by telephone through the Forest Department. The background story was that a Chinese woman had kept him, illegally, at Kuching town, right under our noses!

Nigel looking for in-
sects in the bark of a
tree

Bill really preferred
to stay on the ground
and play with the
other tame animals.
Here he investigates
our otter

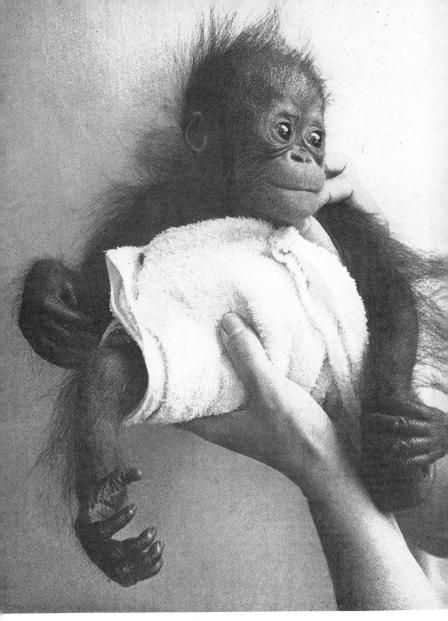

Ossy at $4\frac{1}{2}$ months was our smallest baby

He was a young male and in good shape. He had sixteen teeth with the four fang-teeth to be felt under the gums; thus approximately ten months old. His weight was 12 lb.—just about right for his age. We called him "Derek" for our kind garden-neighbour Derek Jakeway, whose trees, meanwhile, had begun to look very scruffy!

I was delighted at Derek, for Ossy's sake. If Derek proved to be healthy, here was a perfect companion for him, too. Hopefully we gave him Janie's old baby equipment and put him into the new transport cage that had been made for Ossy's journey. When the usual worm- and blood-tests were over, both could share this cage to go overseas.

As the Forest Department's report was very brief, simply stating that a baby Orang had been found in the possession of "one Goh Kui Lan (f), Satok Road, Kuching," and had been seized in accordance with the Wild Life Protection Ordinance, I went to Satok Road in search of Madam Goh. The house was a drab wooden building along a back lane, next to a builder's house. My first attempt to see her was unsuccessful: some Chinese ladies in front of the house told me she was not in. When the same thing happened a few hours later I got suspicious; could I wait for her, I inquired.

I was still negotiating for entry when a door opened. A buxom Chinese woman came directly for me, shouting, glaring.

"I have really had enough of this." Fortunately she spoke the kind of bazaar Malay I could understand well. "First you take *my* baby away, then you say I must pay a *fine* and now you *dare* come and invade my home! Get out, go away!"

I smiled my best smile and soothingly explained to her that I was *not* representing the Forest Department; that I did *not* want to collect a fine; that I was the person chosen to look after her dear little one from now on.

"I want to know how you have been feeding and keeping it, so that there will be no mistake," I said. "Also, how long you have been looking after it and where it came from—if you will tell me."

As she took me in, her word of abuse shifted from accusing me to simply abusing the Forest Officer who had taken the animal away from her the day before. "Imagine the brute," she went on, "he simply took it, saying that I had no right to keep it . . . though I paid 200 dollars for it once ; because I liked it so much, the little animal."

She pointed to an open packing-case in the corner. "This is where he slept ; mind you, only temporarily, because as I say, I don't usually live here but in Sibu, and I have travelled with the little baby all over the place : he got everything—rice, bread, milk, oranges, whatever he liked ; and I carried him around with me *for over a year* !"

I let that implausibility pass, as inspired by her indignation. Apparently she had made use of the little animal to relieve a lot of her repressed feelings, poor dear.

After patient inquiry it came out that approximately six months ago she had bought the animal in a Land Dayak village across the border in Indonesia, near Bau. She did not know who had shot its mother. She had seen it in the *kampong* where she was visiting friends, and they had offered it to her for sale.

"Mind you," she told me, "they said I could sell it at the coast for much more than 200 dollars—that is, what I paid for it —if I offered it to dealers. But I did not want to sell it, I loved it too much !"

This local price was pretty high (all my other orphans had been sold for under twenty dollars), but I did not say so. Probably she had had difficulty in selling the animal before she came to love it so much. I tried to find out more about her methods of feeding instead.

"I gave it milk from a bottle, like to a baby . . ."

"But just now you said rice, and biscuits, and oranges !"

"Yes, of course, milk is not enough for a tiny baby like that."

She explained that she had fed it at irregular times "whenever he felt like it," with "whatever he wanted." That she had taught him to take pulped cooked rice ("*bubor*") from an early age (according to Borneo mothers this is essential to keep a human baby strong and healthy). He had got most of his exercise by clinging to her; but lately she had sometimes allowed it to play outside in the courtyard.

"But then I have been travelling much about the place, always taking him with me," she concluded, "and when I applied for a licence to keep him—that is what they told me I must have to be able to keep him in Sibu—they take the animal away from me and tell me I must pay a fine!"

I consoled her by telling her that she would have been unable to keep the animal for long in a home like hers. That the baby would have doubled his weight and strength, his ability to climb and destroy things within less than a year.

"I have had many Orang babies," I told her, "and they get big and strong quickly. You cannot keep them as pets for long without being cruel to them, even if you love and feed them well!"

I told her about zoos where many animals are kept by people who understand them and treat them well, and that I would find a good place for her baby.

But when I came home and looked at my four charges I suddenly felt guilty and utterly wretched.

IV

Orangs at Sea

The domestic animal follows its master
all over the globe, and has become
thoroughly cosmopolitan. Incidentally I
myself think that there are two types of
psychically constituted human beings,
the cosmopolitan and the home-lover.

Prof. Dr. Heini Hediger,
Zürich, 1955

I

THE BLUE SILHOUETTE OF THE LOW HILL-COUNTRY AT
the western tip of Borneo slowly faded into the South China Sea
and distant morning cloud. It was the 15th May, 1960, and for
over twenty-four hours I had been on board the cargo liner
Socotra, on which I was to travel for many weeks more. I had
boarded ship at the mouth of the Rejang River where it had
anchored alongside mud, mangrove and nipah-palms, loading
timber.

So far I was the only passenger—except, of course, for my
four "children," whom I had in two cages. These were placed
on the boat-deck, sheltered by the lifeboats ; the inner side
permanently warmed by the engine-room. One cage, occupied by
Nigel and Frank, had a shelf and a swing. Uncertain whether I
would get permission to take them out for exercise during the
journey, we had left it large. It was very heavy, with a floor and
frame of "ironwood" timber and wire-mesh walls and roof. We
had had great difficulty in shifting it from the small launch which
had taken us from Kuching alongside *Socotra*, over a series of
small Chinese craft that were crowding round the big liner at the
anchorage, into the grips of the ship's crane. The other cage
was smaller and lighter. It had two baskets strung up inside ;
these were the sleeping "nests" for Ossy and Derek. Both cages
stood on low feet to make washing-down easy. For the night—
and for additional shelter from wind, rain or sun—I brought a
large supply of ready-made Malay palm-leaf shelter to be wrapped
round the cages as required.

All four animals had been terribly excited by their first trip
over the water, strange surroundings and many people on board
a ship. As long as we had been loading, a crowd of Chinese and
Dayak workmen had collected at every free moment to see
them closely, so that I had fenced the cages off with a long rope

139

and had myself sat in the enclosure as "guard." I could not have people sneezing or spitting near my Orangs ! The noise of winches and cranes had continued until the early morning hours, and Nigel and Frank did not go to sleep until after midnight. But as we had started moving at sunrise, all was well.

As I was relaxing luxuriously in a deck-chair, Captain Nowell came to inspect. I pointed out Nigel and Frank and introduced Ossy and Derek, whom I held in my arms. They looked somewhat disdainfully at his smart white uniform.

"I hope you will not object to my taking them out of their cages at times," I said as casually as I could ; "they will not be naughty—I promise you !"

He got the point immediately. "Well, *they* seem all right," he poked at Ossy in a friendly way, "but what about the big ones? Will they behave ? Can you really control them ?"

For a moment I had awful visions of Nigel and Frank "escaping"—climbing up masts and down funnels. But quickly I thought of the alternative agony : for them to stay in their cage for weeks on end.

"Of course I can control them," I said. "I have been looking after them for years and I know what to do !" He smiled.

"All right, then . . . let's see what happens. But don't take any chances, it's your responsibility."

We discussed matters of food supply—fresh fruit which I would have to get at the various ports—and the help of one man to clean the cages and feed the animals. It is impossible for one person to do the cleaning and watch at the same time. And in case I was sick—I am not a very bright sailor—someone else must know what to do.

"Our senior cadet officer, Cliff Purchese, is very good with animals. He has been looking after dogs and horses, and even a load of water-buffaloes we had on board between Bangkok and Manila !"

I remembered that when I had been searching for a passage to England, a good friend in Singapore, Charles Letts, the

managing director of Jardine Waugh, had helped me. It was he
who had found this P. & O. ship. One condition, though, had
been made :

SOCOTRA CAPTAIN CABLED ORANGS ACCEPTABLE PRO-
VIDING COMPATIBLE WITH DOGS ALREADY BOOKED (.)
HAVE CONFIRMED COMPATIBILITY—CHARLES

I had visualised a pack of greyhounds chasing along the
decks.

"Tell me, Captain, what about those dogs you are carrying.
I have not seen them anywhere."

"They will be coming along, I guess, but they will be in
charge of their owners." He told me one was a boxer, the other
a dachshund. Relief !

"One thing I should like to suggest," the captain said, turning
away, "I think it will be better to transfer the cages to the cor-
responding position on the starboard side. We may run into
monsoon in the Indian Ocean and it will be better to have them
on the "posh" side. There they will be protected. We can do
that in Singapore."

I thanked him—little realising how important the transfer
would prove to be in the days to come.

I had a session with Cliff Purchese later. We went to the cool-
room to store the supply of fruit, and I explained that it was
important not to feed fresh from the cooler. We saw the ship's
baker, who was to give us one fresh loaf daily. Then we stored
away spare sacks, ropes and palm-leaf. We went to the cadet's
pantry, where I would prepare the babies' bottles. I wrote down
feeding times and amounts for each of the animals. We agreed
that I would feed the babies and he would feed Nigel and Frank.
The cleaning was for both of us, early every morning.

"We shall see how it goes with exercise." I told Cliff that
the captain had agreed we take them out, "but I want to be
careful at first, until they know you."

Cliff was tall and slim. His hair was fair. He had blue eyes; he was just the opposite of Bidai. But like Bidai, he was one of those men who understand animals. Nigel and Frank were friendly to him from the start.

"You must be calm and of good temper," I told him. "Of course they *can* bite horribly if they want to, but they never have and they won't start now if you show them what kind of person you really are."

We took Nigel and Frank by the hand for a walk along the deck in the vicinity of the cages, giving them a chance to investigate to their heart's content.

"To-morrow we'll let them walk about on their own. Once they are better used to the place and more relaxed, there is less danger that they will suddenly dash off."

As if to illustrate the point, the ship's siren let off its deep, penetrating roar. Frank climbed up me in fright, cuddling my chest, Nigel nearly tore Cliff's arm out in his sudden urge to get away.

It was noon. The coastline of Borneo had disappeared. The South China Sea was unruffled, the colour of lead. We took Nigel and Frank back to their cage; it was feeding time.

2

On the 24th May—a hot day, even at sea—we were anchored off the Sumatran shore, waiting to be taken into Belawan port. The coast with its distant outline of hills, its bordering fringe of mangrove swamp and the small fishing craft operating at the mouth of the Deli River, looked very much the same as Borneo.

The Sumatran forests are the second remaining territory of Orang-utans. Sumatran Orangs are better known in zoos and are usually referred to as being "bigger and of lighter colour" than Borneo Orangs, though the difference is slight and variations occur widely. The belief that Sumatran Orangs are much bigger was probably inspired by the fact that the first large-scale exports of *adult* Orangs took place from Sumatra. Some of these were impressive males with broad cheek callosities and huge arm-spans —quite unlike the few specimens zoo people had hitherto been able to see.

Some had even been shipped from the port of Belawan, where we were now waiting. They had all been trapped in the Province of Atchin, Northern Sumatra. All by one man in the late twenties Mijheer van Goens.

Van Goens decided that he could—which indeed he did— make a fortune by developing a monopoly in trapping and selling Orangs on a large scale. Only a few adult specimens had been shown in Europe between 1893 and 1895; all of them had died quickly, and zoo people were thoroughly discouraged. Their record of longevity was thirteen weeks !

In 1926 van Goens captured his first adult Sumatran Orang, a male, and exported him. He was sold by the German dealer, Ruhe, to Dresden Zoo for not less than 20,000 marks, which was then worth £4,000. "Goliath" (this was his name) became famous amongst zoo people because Dresden Zoo managed to keep him alive for over two years (he died of "old age"). He is referred to by Ruhe as the "trial Orang"—because his success immediately caused three large-scale imports of over 100 Orangs during 1927-28, from Sumatra. Professor Brandes describes him thus :

"Since 1895 no such giant Orang had been imported and I was very reluctant to acquire this expensive specimen which was offered to me by the dealer Ruhe of Alfeld.

But the animal's apparent good health and the impressive sight of its wonderful fur convinced me and I bought it even though it might live as little as six or perhaps at most thirteen weeks as his four predecessors. But now it has lived for two years and one and a half months and was always well except during its very last days. . . . *Had Goliath died, like his predecessors within a matter of weeks, the widespread opinion*

*that it is impossible to keep adult Orang-utans in captivity would
have been confirmed and the large imports of the past two years
which have given many German zoos the attraction of an Orang
family, would not have taken place."*[1]

Although Professor Brandes contributed to the knowledge
about Orangs and his deep understanding helped others to treat
the animals more successfully in captivity (as we shall see in the
next chapter) it would probably have been better for the Orangs'
sake had the "trial Orang," Goliath, been sold to someone else,
to an ignorant man ; and then had died quickly. For what took
place in Sumatra in 1927-28 on a large scale was against any
conservation principles or human decencies of even a Dutch
colony thirty years ago !

The dealer Ruhe describes the events without apparent concern.
Main interest was the profitable sale of Orangs ("The amount of
animals that I told van Goens he should trap was *unlimited* ; I
did not want to be *too optimistic* . . .") :[2]

"Van Goens seemed a wizard. There were numerous theories
about his methods of trapping. Somebody said that he gave
drugs and doctored bananas to the animals, subsequently
simply collecting them at their sleeping places—of course a
quite unfounded story. Others reported of very unpleasant
methods. What Goens actually did was to encircle a wide area
by a great number of native helpers. Round the centre where
the apes crowded that had not managed to get away, he felled
clear a circular space so that the animals had no way of escape.
Hunger slowly drove them into the strong nets he erected
with particularly appetising baits. But catching families of
apes in his nets was not necessarily the same as having them
in his bag. One often underestimates the strength of apes,
especially when they are fully grown. Many of the Orang-

[1] Prof. G. Brandes, Dresden, 29.12.28, in *Der Zoologische Garten*
Vol. I, 1929. [My italics].

[2] H. Ruhe in *Wilde Tiere frei Haus*, Munich, 1960.

utans succeeded in tearing the strong nets and escaping at the last minute. But a certain number usually ended in the transport cages.

"All this happened in Atchin in northern Sumatra . . ."[1]

The first transport of twenty-five animals arrived in Europe in April, 1927. It is not known how many were injured or killed during the trapping or if there were any losses at sea. Ruhe simply tells us of the arrival of twenty-five; that they were "quiet" when they emerged from the heavy ironwood cages. Whole families appeared: fathers, mothers and babies—even some males with broad cheeks! Ruhe made wonderful business and sold out at once. In fact, interested zoo directors had come in crowds to Alfeld, a small town near Hanover, to see and choose their own specimens on arrival. A sort of modern slave-market ensued.

Only one of the party, an artist, not a zoo man, was deeply moved by the sight of the Orangs. Ruhe missed him when his wife called for lunch. He found him in front of the Orangs' cages. The man was annoyed at being pulled away.

"Don't talk!" he said. "The animals are looking at me so!" He came reluctantly, so as not to offend the lady of the house. He was silent (Ruhe notes in surprise) for the rest of the day.

The second group transport came in a few months later. Again, it is impossible to reconstruct the full story now. Ruhe tells us that a total of thirty-three Orangs arrived at Rotterdam in August, 1927, and that they were all sold to an American dealer, John Ringling of circus fame. A quarrel ensued between the two dealers, because two of the animals died during the transport over the Atlantic. Ringling refused to pay the whole price.

When the third transport reached Europe in 1928, the excitement had worn off. No crowds of zoo directors now awaited the Orangs. Naturally it was still good business, though:

"The third transport with forty-four animals did not last long
[1] op. cit.

. . . The buyers came and went and soon all animals had been sold. To many European countries and to other parts of the world."

Ruhe adds somewhat regretfully :

"Unfortunately there were no more Orang deliveries for the present. I cannot say definitely whether Mijnheer van Goens's trappings—which were all sold through me—had been the reason for the enactment of a new law by which trappings and export of Orang-utans were strictly forbidden—a law which is still valid to-day !"[1]

The enforcement of this law was, and still is, ineffective. Shooting of Orangs, to obtain their bodies as specimens, or their babies for sale, continues indiscriminately to this day. Ruhe mentions Sumatra as the source of Orangs in 1929-30 ; an adult Orang is priced 12,000 marks in his sales list of 1930. Though he was perhaps the main dealer in Germany during those years, there were others in other parts of the world quick to learn that profits in the Orang business were high.

In contrast to the native population, "white" travellers and hunters have always been particularly insensitive in their encounters with Orang in the jungle. Gustav Schneider, for instance, a German naturalist, tells in a scientific publication how he collected and studied Orangs in 1897-9 in Sumatra :

"The natives told me . . . that in the jungle near Darat was a pregnant Mais who moved much on the jungle floor owing to her condition. For three days I searched for this rare prey. Finally, about 5 p.m. I saw her on a low bush-tree and shot her through shoulder and lungs. At this moment I saw something fly high over my head. My servants and I thought it was a broken branch because Orangs often defend themselves by throwing them at you, and took no notice. When I looked at my prey I saw that she had already given birth and gave

[1] H. Ruhe in *Wilde Tiere frei Haus*, Munich, 1960.

away milk, but the young one was not with her or anywhere near. Only then did I look for the object thrown away earlier. After a long search we found, about fifteen metres away in the undergrowth, a delicate wrinkled creature, its hair still wet with fruit-water. It was 40 cm. long and alive; it survived although it had been grazed by a bullet. What we had taken for a branch was in fact the child which the deadly wounded mother had tried to rescue in this way. Surely a remarkable trait in the emotional life of an Orang-utan."[1]

Those were white men's early efforts in Sumatra. Van Goens and scores of others have since feathered their manly nests in complete disregard of the animals.

As we were waiting for a cargo of palm oil alongside Belawan's concrete jetty, three young Malays turned up at the gangway and called to the ship's crew. They were leading a baby Gibbon on a thin rope and wanted to sell it.

It was a male, about a year old, with a sweet black face and light grey fur. But there were dreadful sores on neck and belly; it was in an apathetic state and it was plain to see that it could not survive the journey, even if someone bought it.

"Five dollars—Straits money! You buy!"

They pressed the dirty string into my hand; the animal sat hunched up, covered with flies.

"He nice, sweet animal—very tame! You buy!"

I felt like hitting them, but they would not have understood. I turned away and went back to the ship. I was longing to be at sea, even if sick.

[1] G. Schneider, "Ergebnisse Zoologischer Forschungsreisen in Sumatra"; *Zool. Jahrb.* (Syst.) 23, 1906.

3

On the evening of the 23rd June, *Socotra* was rounding the north-western tip of Sumatra and steamed out of the Malacca Straits into the setting sun. The Indian Ocean heaved the ship up and down on a low swell. The monsoon wind blew stiffly from the south-west and the sky was cloudless.

We were to see nothing but water for eight or nine days. The night was warm in spite of the wind and I felt just right in a light summer dress. Before going in to dinner I checked the cages to see if all was well. Nigel lay on his side, snoring; Frank was crouched on his belly embracing a sack; and the babies breathed regularly, deeply asleep in their baskets behind palm-leaf walls. For the first time Cliff had tied down the cages to the deck with thick ropes, as if he was expecting bad weather. I dreaded bad sea; and how would the Orangs take it?

We were eleven human passengers, four Orangs and one dog. A large boxer had come on board in Singapore with a family of four—Mr. and Mrs. Holliday and their grown-up daughters.

A large crate, equipped with sleeping platform, brocade-covered feather cushion and the name "Jerry" on the door had been tied to the boat-deck. But the dog refused to sleep in it. He made such a row the first night he was left inside that one of the family had to watch over him every night from then on, sleeping beside him on deck in a chair. This was all right as long as we were in the tropics, when the cabins were hot and stuffy. It was often nicer to spend the night outside, in a chair, under the moon. But I wondered how they would keep it up with bad weather!

Mrs. Holliday walked the deck with Jerry and she stopped to ask about my children.

"They are never afraid of the dog, you know, and one of the babies often pokes a finger at him when he puts his nose near the wire—yet Jerry is so much bigger!"

This was, of course, Ossy. He was unafraid and trusting, where Derek was cautious and shy. If strange people came near and I was not there, Derek clung to Ossy instead, gripping tightly with both arms round his small body. His fear and tension were often extreme and were probably caused by his foster-mother of old, she who had treated him like the baby she wanted to have but never had!

I asked Mrs. Holliday what she intended to do with her pet in bad weather.

"One of us will always have to stay with him, I suppose—he can't bear to be alone." She petted the dog and he wagged his stump tail. "Though it seems so silly," she added, "because he will have to go into quarantine for *six months* once we get to England! This will be real cruel for him—though I will be able to go and see him often!"

We discussed the subject and then she said:

"I don't know how you can bear to part with your animals and give them away—especially the babies! What will they do without you?"

She was not the first person to ask this rather obvious question. What people meant was: "What will *you* do without them?"

Why is it that so many animal-lovers expect their pets to respond emotionally like humans, and will not let an animal live in its own particular way—a dog like a dog and bird like a bird? It was my responsibility to find a good home for my Orangs where they could live as happily as was possible, developing independently and learning to cope with a new life and with mankind in particular. My own feelings should not matter as far as the Orangs were concerned; and it was entirely my own business to deal with them myself.

"They will love a new mother very easily," I said to Mrs. Holliday, "provided that I disappear completely. The babies still need one. They will adopt the next best person, as there is no alternative."

But she thought this was cruel.

It was rough the next morning. Grey clouds hung low over the water. The ship tossed and pitched in every direction. A strong wind blew from south-west. The cages were well sheltered on starboard and we cleaned them as usual. Cliff worked with hose and brush. When they were clean he put a new supply of dry sacks and straw inside. Meanwhile I watched Nigel and Frank, an exhausting task. As soon as the door of their cage was opened, they dashed out, ran along the boat-deck chasing each other, looked for screws to unscrew, tackle to untackle. When they were fed up with the deck they started climbing up into the lifeboats. This was much worse, for here was a wonderful supply of emergency kit : matches and oil, bandages and all sorts of surgical material, dry rations of biscuits, fish-hooks, even a cooking stove, cans and pans—most of it neatly wrapped and packed : a paradise for an investigating ape whose main and untiring interest is probing and taking things to bits.

It was agony to keep up with the two Orangs popping in and out of a series of four boats each of them equipped thus. To throw out one you had to climb up into the boat yourself. Once up you would discover the other sticking his head out from a boat farther along. They thought it was a fine game to chase and be chased in that way.

Cliff's attempts at education were unsuccessful. For some days running he tried to put whoever was naughty straight back into the cage. Obviously neither Frank nor Nigel was able to interpret this novel human reaction correctly. They screamed to be let out until we felt sorry for them—and then the game could continue.

For some time, exhausted by the attempts to lure Frank and Nigel away from the boats, Cliff and I had been very slack. We did not take the trouble to check and cover up when the morning's exercise was over. The blast came when the captain, on one of his inspection rounds, got it into his head to climb into one of the boats himself. He hardly believed what he saw !

Although I myself had the good fortune not to meet him before dinner, when the worst of his indignation had cooled off, poor Cliff met with a severe reprimand. For several days both Frank and Nigel were in the ship's bad books. We watched them very carefully from then on, and always tidied up after them. But it took nearly five weeks of sea-journey for them to lose interest in the boats, and then mainly because they found something else, more exciting, even bigger and better.

On that first day of rough seas I had a very hard time indeed. First of all I thought I had better hold on to their hands, because I was frightened they might feel sea-sick, lose balance and topple overboard. But although I had some trouble myself to walk upright on the swaying deck, they seemed completely unconcerned and there was no question of them losing *their* balance. After I had slithered headlong twice, holding on to their hands, I gave up and let them do as they pleased. They delighted in the movement of the ship, and paid no attention to the occasional spray breaking over the sides.

The babies took their bottles. But we had to leave their cage covered because of the wind and spray, and by the time the morning cleaning and exercise was over I felt thoroughly seasick. There was no question of breakfast—I took to my bunk for the rest of the day, asking Cliff to do the feeding and caring.

I woke up at night, when I was thrown off my bunk. I was frightened and got up to look at the cages, to make sure that they were safely tied and dry. I was determined to rescue the babies and secretly take them into my cabin if I found them in any way miserable. It took some time to cross over the swaying deck and reach the cages. They had not moved an inch and they were perfectly dry. The air inside was warm and all four animals were breathing regularly. The position was the only sheltered one, however. Just for fun I went round to the port side, where they had been before. Gushes of wind, rain, and sea swept the deck, in spite of the lifeboats, and it was quite cold. It would not have been possible for the animals to stand up to the weather here, even in covered cages!

Gingerly I made my way back to my cabin. I met the watch on the steps, balancing a steaming cup of tea.

"First Officer told me to get it for Mrs. Holliday," he said, grinning. "She has been sitting outside her cabin with the dog in that weather *all night* !"

It was the thin edge of the wedge for both her and me.

4

Though all four Orangs stood up to the weather well, their health started to deteriorate, with bouts of diarrhoea and sneezing, as the monsoon wind and rain kept on sweeping the decks. They had too little exercise and became bored and miserable.

On the 11th June, when the Somaliland coast came into view, suddenly the misery ended. Next day we were floating on the calm waters of the Gulf of Aden, in full sunshine. Now was the time for a general clean-up. We had not dared to wash the animals for several days as there was no way of getting their fur dry. They looked filthy, all of them. I discovered that we had run out of sweet water on deck ; only a tiny trickle came from the hose, not even a bucketful !

I took the babies to the cadet's pantry, which had a sink for washing dishes. Both Ossy and Derek loved sitting in the luke-warm water and being shampooed. I rubbed them down and took them back into the sun. They spent the whole morning outside the cage, climbing around my deck-chair and the railing. They took more milk for their meals than on any of the previous days.

It was not so easy with Frank and Nigel. They were much too big for the sink, and I had no permission to use a bathroom. Cliff took pity on them !

"I'll take them to the cadets' showers—*they* won't mind !"

He took them down and washed them under the shower. They stole the soap and tried to eat it. They loved the water and opened their mouths wide to catch it !

Meanwhile a small army of sailors was spring-cleaning the decks, scrubbing the planks, on their hands and knees, with flat sandstone. Frank was very interested and got hold of a stone. One of the sailors hopefully gave it to him (perhaps he could take over the job ?), but he only chewed and bit it, poked it with his fingers. Although I demonstrated to him what to do, holding his hand in mine as I rubbed the stone up and down the planks, he did not get the point. (Orangs seldom do—and we never tried to teach them tricks.) Similarly Nigel showed a keen interest, but only in the stone itself. After biting, chewing and poking it, he threw it down on the deck.

One morning, during exercise time, I lost Nigel. Frank had run into forbidden country for a moment with me chasing after him. Nigel took the chance to disappear. We looked for him all over : the lifeboats, the roof, round the funnels—no good ! Then we started frantically searching inside, visualising the terrible things he could do wherever he went. We found him in the engineers' shower. A helpful sailor had put on the water for him. He stood there upright with his mouth wide open in sheer delight !

The sailors said he had climbed down a hatch slowly, looking carefully about him. He had explored the gangway and walked into the nearest cabin, which happened to be the second engineer's. He had taken a short look round, grabbed a towel from the rack near the wash-basin, draped it round his neck, and thus attired had sat down on a chair. The Indian steward, who was just cleaning the cabin, had run away screaming. Nigel had taken a glass that he found on the table, and then stopped for a moment to admire himself in the mirror over the wash-basin— towel, glass and all. Then he had calmly walked out of the cabin, glass in hand, and into the shower. By now he had an audience of delighted sailors. They put on the water for him and that is how we found him. Nigel was properly conscious of his performance and from now on we had to watch that hatch. He managed to get away three or four times, either making for the shower or for the second engineer's cabin. Unfortunately, of course, the word got round. The time had come for a second ticking off.

As there were no branches and leaves for Nigel and Frank to play with, they took other things as substitutes. Ropes were conveniently coiled round their bodies in a wide circle, as if to outline a nest platform. Screws and wire, rags and bits of straw were then placed inside, shifted and turned round. Another favourite but more elaborate game was the "hankie contest." They got hold of a handkerchief and each of them placed it on top of his head with the sides hanging over the eyes. For a short moment the animal sat like this, blindfolded, opposite the other, who would then rush forward to tear the hankie from his face and make him "see"—and then place the hankie on his own head, covering his eyes.

One day as we were nearing Suez, with the rugged bare mountains of Saudi Arabia outlined in the distance, I sat on a deck-chair near the cages with the babies playing around me.

I suddenly jumped: a large, winged insect had landed on my lap. A few more crawled on deck: pink locusts that had swarmed out to sea. One found its way into Nigel's and Frank's cage; crawled about the upper sitting shelf. Nigel looked at it fascinated, but did not touch or smell it. Frank moved up to the high shelf and got into "attack position," standing on all fours. He bashed at it with one fist, squashing it down. As it hopped and buzzed in an effort to get away, he started pulling at its wings. He took it up in his hands, held it to his face for the smell, and quickly bit the large head off. He chewed it for some time and played with the headless corpse. Perhaps he did not like the taste much, because he never ate the rest. Nigel remained an interested spectator throughout.

Certainly neither of them had ever seen a pink locust before. Each animal had dealt with the situation in its own way. Had they been hungry, they might have eaten it. As it was, they had expressed their keen curiosity and desire to try out things. They had approached the insect with caution, tried and rejected it as not much good. Nigel had left Frank to do the "donkey work" of the investigation.

5

The day we were due to pass Gibraltar—we had been on board six weeks—the end of the journey seemed near. I did not realise that the worst was still to come.

The Mediterranean voyage had been uneventful. Hugging the African coast we travelled due west once more. Watches were set back for the last time and people started asking questions on the exact time of arrival at London docks. I was worried by the weather. Though the last days of June should have been graced by sunshine and warmth, we never seemed to get away from a stiff, cold wind. Many days before, I had shifted the babies' cage aft, and it was now better sheltered. I often crouched with the babies in secluded places on deck in small patches of sun. There was not enough room for the large cage to be shifted ; and the only way of dealing with the situation was to leave the palm-leaf and tarpaulin sheets on during day-time as well, which meant that Nigel and Frank had to sit in the dark. Their hands and feet were often cold—a sure sign that they did not feel as comfortable as they should. Frank developed a slight cold. On the afternoon of 24th June, as we passed Gibraltar, the weather deteriorated further.

I went to see Captain Nowell, to tell him that unless the weather improved, I should have to seek alternative accommodation for my charges under deck. Where could I put them ?

"I'm afraid there is nothing I can do," he explained sympathetically, "there is nowhere to put them. The hold is too draughty and you would not be able to go and feed them there easily. There is no room anywhere to accommodate live animals except on deck."

This was an unexpected blow. I had visualised it an easy

matter to transfer the cages inside ; but now I was told that none of the usual cargo liners on the Far East run had accommodation for live animals except on deck. He asked me if there was serious danger for my charges.

"Most definitely, yes, for all four of them !" I told him how easily they can catch cold, leading to fatal pneumonia, especially with the babies, and that Orangs are very susceptible to all sorts of bronchial infection and respiratory diseases in particular.

"It would be most unfortunate for anything like that to happen after all this time on board. By the way, did you hear on the radio the report that hundreds of monkeys died on a transport at sea ? They blamed the Captain !"

We settled down to a cold beer and he told me about it. There had been a shipment of a thousand monkeys sent on a cargo boat, from India to Europe. Over six hundred of the animals died of pneumonia en route and the crew of the ship had been blamed for the disaster. They had "petted the animals too fondly," the story went ; and had thereby carried the disease from one cage to the other !

"But that's absurd . . . how can the crew be blamed when a thousand monkeys are exposed on deck !" I thought of the monsoon-swept weather-side. "They must have been put all over the place and those in the worst positions probably died during the first stages of the journey !"

Nobody had accompanied the shipment. The owner of the cargo had simply placed the animals on board—heavily insured, of course. The crew had fed the animals and cleaned the cages on the voyage.

The captain went on : "If anybody is to blame as far as the ship goes, it is the captain. It is he who accepted the cargo without a skilled person to look after the animals. I would not have agreed . . . although it is difficult to refuse, once the company asks you to accept a cargo."

It was the old story : the seller of the animals, a dealer and business man, was simply interested to make money. He did not care what became of the animals, so long as they were safely insured. What happened to them on the way, whether they died of exposure or "excessive petting," whether they ended up in a zoo, museum, circus or laboratory, was unimportant.

"I would not have accepted your animals without you to accompany them," the captain said, "and I am very much put out now you tell me you can't look after them properly if the weather deteriorates. Because it is *going* to deteriorate, I'm afraid. So we must try and do something about it."

He took me to look around for various possibilities. The cages were too large to be placed anywhere inside, except in the hold; but I convinced myself, and him, that this was even worse than the deck. The best solution was a cabin into which we could put the animals without the cage; and Captain Nowell decided on the "cargo office." This was a small cabin equipped with a desk, sofa and cupboard. He said I could have it, strip it and put Nigel and Frank inside as soon as I thought it too cold on deck.

For the babies we chose a small corridor on deck which we sealed off with plywood and tarpaulins. In this we placed their cage; rigged two sun-burners for warmth and light. It was very cosy. Cliff called it "the cave."

All was ready before nightfall. As the wind and sea were becoming steadily worse, I decided to move Nigel and Frank right away. After the evening meal of milk and fruit—now consisting of oranges, apples and a few water-melons which had somehow survived since Singapore—we took them all into the cargo office, with a supply of sacks and straw.

I won't forget that particular night: it was full of excitement, and not only for Nigel and Frank. Naturally, they did not go to sleep for a long time and were still busily exploring their new home when I looked through the window before going in to dinner. Frank had discovered that he could shut peeping sailors out: the watchman told me that every time he took a look through the window, Frank pulled up the sunshade from inside with a big bang. When I came to look, however, Frank pressed his nose and lips tightly against the glass and showed delight when I did the same to him from the other side.

After dinner I checked again. Both slept soundly in a corner on sacks. But I saw, with horror, that meanwhile the central heating system had been torn off the walls. The pipes were bent, the whole fixed apparatus hung at a crazy angle, while chipped-off plaster and paint covered the floor ! I visualised another row with the captain in the morning.

Later that night, I was wakened by loud shouts. Two human passengers were having a terrific marital row. The wife spent the rest of the night in my bed, holding my hand. The captain sorted out the mess next morning. When I came to tell him about the damage Frank and Nigel had done in his cargo office, he only smiled and said :

"Even *people* go round the bend if they live on a ship for long without much to do ! I don't blame your charges—in fact, I understand them only too well."

The sea was rough and it was freezing cold. Presently the foghorn began to blow. We had been on board altogether too long.

6

Some days later I was on deck in a sheltered corner as we steamed up the River Thames. I was hugging both babies under my woollen coat, which I had fished out from the bottom of my suitcase. They were peeping at the banks of the river, fascinated, their little black eyes settling on ships, houses and trees. For weeks they had seen nothing but water. This was a wonderful change. I was full of apprehension. The time had come to say good-bye ; the adventure was over.

By evening they were due to go on the train to Edinburgh, and to arrive at their new home next morning. Nigel and Frank were to be transhipped to Hamburg. None of them had had a bath for days. I had obtained special permission from the Chief Engineer to use his own private shower for a thorough clean-up before arrival, but had given up the idea because it was too cold.

ORANGS AT SEA

The cargo office was a shambles ; they had hardly been able to leave it since we had put them in.

The main worry had been to keep the babies warm. The two sun-burners were on in "the cave" day and night and the place was warm. But the babies had to get out at times for fresh air. There was also some danger of fire, so that the watch peeped into the den every few hours. I spent my time checking and fussing. My last entry in this journey's diary reads :

"29.6.60 : night and early morning terrific gale, bitterly cold. This is the end ! At 7 a.m. Frank's chill seems improved, the babies feel cold, but are healthy. Arrival London docks due 4 p.m."

Tom, who had travelled by air, and my stepson Max were both waiting on the wharf as we came alongside at London docks. Max climbed aboard like an Orang-utan before the gangway was up. He handed me a roll of film which I urgently needed. And somebody else was there : Joan and Janie Merry, now on leave, who had come down from the north of England to meet their old baby, Ossy.

The ship that should have taken Nigel and Frank on to Hamburg the same day had already left, for we had been several hours late owing to the weather. The appointed agents had found a substitute, but the animals could not be transferred for another twenty-four hours. Cliff kindly agreed to look after them until then and I went up to the captain, the babies in my arms, to say good-bye.

I thanked him and asked him how much I owed him for damages in the cargo office.

"Get out !" he said jokingly. "Get out and go away ! I hope I will never carry again such little devils as yours."

Ossy and Derek enjoyed tremendously the taxi ride through London, to the animal hospital at Regent's Park Zoo, which took them in as guests for a few hours until it was time to go on the night train to Edinburgh. For the last time I gave them their evening bottle, settled them in their cage, covered them with their little blankets and told them to go to sleep. I asked for a dark cover to be put over the cage so that they were not disturbed by the strange surroundings. For a little while I remained outside and, aware of my presence, they soon settled down.

I tiptoed out to drive to my hotel. They would wake up to find a new mother. . . .

Journey's end was more dramatic for Nigel and Frank. It involved trouble at my as well as at their end. Hagenbeck, Hamburg, had cabled they wanted the animals accompanied from London to Hamburg by a responsible person. I was ready to go with them. I had been at sea so long that I did not object to a couple of days more, even though it might be rough! But Tom was determined: "It's either *me* or *them*. Please yourself and choose. I certainly don't agree that you go. You have done enough. Find somebody else."

Even loving husbands are sometimes very unfeeling and I had no alternative. An agent hunted all over London to find a person to take Nigel and Frank to Hamburg. He found a charming old Danish gentleman—a retired sea-lion tamer!

It took a whole morning to transfer the large cage to a small cargo vessel, the *Fink*, due to leave next day for Hamburg. The *Fink* had ideal accommodation—a special compartment inside the hold, heated from one side by the engines. Its opening on deck was not quite large enough to take the big cage: we had to knock in corners and door to get it inside. We hung sun-burners for light and warmth, so Nigel and Frank were really snug—no matter what the weather was like outside.

I brought a selection of fruit to the *Fink*: strawberries, cherries and gooseberries—both for a last real treat and to see what they did with this new food.

After an exercise along the docks I put them into their cage on board the new ship. The sea-lion tamer was a great success: they playfully stole his spectacles and tore a hole in his coat when he said hallo. Only afterwards did he confess that he had never had anything to do with Orangs before !

They loved the new fruit and gorged themselves with it, especially the strawberries. I poked my hands through the wire.

"Good-bye, children, it's for good this time. I hope you will be happy."

I walked back to the road, among the piled boxes and cranes and the boisterous dockyard activities of men and machines. It was just as well I had a long way to go. I did not want to speak. I felt defeated. In spite of all efforts and understanding, I had not been able to do better than to expose them to an uncertain fate in a zoo. I was sorry I had loved them so well and would miss them. I hoped that they would grow up to become happy zoo animals.

I made up my mind there and then to go and see them before returning to Sarawak, to make sure all was well.

V

Orangs in Zoos

In the course of the negotiations which
led to the formation of the Zoological
Society of London a prospectus was prepared and circulated in 1825, which contains this passage : "It would well become
Britain to offer another, and a very
different series of exhibitions to the
population of her metropolis ; namely,
animals brought from every part of the
globe to be applied either to some useful
purpose, or as objects of scientific research, not vulgar admiration." This
statement contains the substance of the
guiding principle on which all zoological
gardens should be conducted. The best
zoos are those which have in fact adhered
to this aim.

Geoffrey Schomberg, F.Z.S.,
London, 1957

When Janie gave him his milk, Ossy would drink 6 or 7 oz. without stopping, and immediately fall asleep

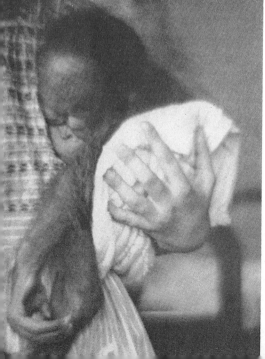

At sea. *Above*, here, as everywhere, Frank was always climbing.
Below, Nigel and Frank at their handkerchief game

TO MANY PEOPLE WHO ARE FOND OF ANIMALS AND HAVE perhaps observed some in the wild, it is a sad affair to go to a zoo. Yet nowadays a zoo is the only place where people leading a "civilised" existence in crowded towns may see or have any contact with wild animals.

Most zoos have evolved during the past fifty years from an animal prison where individual specimens were kept on view in small lockers, to a park with wide open enclosures where animal groups roam about freely and naturally. Some zoos are already completely transformed ; others are still in the process of doing so ; we may see an old-fashioned tiny cage housing a bear or a tiger—a pitiful and often shocking sight—next to a wonderful open basin for sea-elephants and sea-lions. How much of the transformation has been achieved mostly depends on organisation and money, with emphasis on the former. An active zoo director draws interest and goodwill, as well as the large crowds to bring in the cash. But where a director or committee is contented merely to carry out their administration duties, nothing much happens for years.

Unhappily, the building of an ape-house to conform with modern ideas is an expensive affair. At many zoos this has been the argument against a new one as long as an old house was standing. Even in famous zoos with large resources, the modernisation of the ape-house or the building of a new one is often put at the bottom of the list as a matter least urgent or needing "slight improvement" only—as for instance the erection of glass walls in the inner part of the house to shield the animals from infection by visitors. As often as not, even if a new ape-house is built, it lacks expansive imaginative outdoor facilities, for instance, a place without bars where the animals have freedom, and incentive, to exercise and play. It does seem that in this human beings are least sensitive to the requirements of their nearest relatives, the apes !

Yet it is apes and monkeys that most zoo visitors want to see above all else. Their cage areas are crowded at all times ; and this is true all over the world. Zoos are quite ready to spend large sums for the acquisition of new specimens, even to organise elaborate trapping expeditions—specially for Gorilla and Orang-utan. But then they house their costly prizes in cages and under conditions where they have little chance of surviving for more than a few years. The prestige of being able to show a "complete collection of apes" has become more important to some zoos, than the survival of the animals themselves.

Regent's Park Zoo in London—perhaps the most famous of all zoos—still retains an old-fashioned ape-house. Though many alterations have taken place in the past few decades and extensive modernisation is planned for the near future, none of it has so far favoured the apes. There is a series of barred cages (outdoors and indoors) ; each compartment has a floor-space of roughly 500 square feet, a concrete floor, sometimes a metal swing. There is *no* other equipment; no toys, no swinging ropes, nothing to stimulate interest and activity, let alone intelligence, happiness, zest and the feel of decent living.

Here the apes' fun and games of the day consist of begging for food and performing tricks, such as spitting and urinating at spectators and clapping of hands (Chimpanzees) ; begging for food or staying hidden for hour after hour in a bunch of horse straw (Orang-utan) ; sitting stoically in front of the visitors for hours on end without moving (Gorilla). As hardly any visitor (and seldom a zoo director) has ever observed apes in the wild, there can be little conception of how far this exhibit is a distorted, farcical picture of what once were apes, long ago and far away, in their homelands.

I cannot tell in what way captivity affects Gorilla and Chim-panzee, as I have never myself been fortunate enough to study them in the wild. I cannot say whether they should ideally have a wide-open area, a sand-pit, living trees or rocks to climb. Their requirements are different from the Orang's because they mainly live on the ground. In London Zoo the reflection comes to mind, though, that it seems contrary to any idea of conservation or kindness to keep a Gorilla in constant solitary confinement; and that lack of exercise, coupled with constant feeding by visitors, cannot lead to much good.

Orangs live in trees. Their strong arms are made to swing from swaying branches; their feet to grip and climb, not to walk on the ground. Yet they generally get the same sort of facilities and treatment in zoos as *terrestrial* Gorillas and Chimpanzees. Often they are kept in one cage with the latter—to the overwhelming disadvantage of the Orangs. To a certain extent young Orangs adapt themselves to walking on concrete. But once they get older they usually grow resigned to sitting on an upper shelf (if there is one). By that time, the rough surface of the floor, or wrong diet, or disease, have rendered their long, shiny hair dull and sparse, moth-eaten and short. Some Orangs appear entirely "naked" and their fur never grows again. In the wild—or in Pig Lane—such pitiful creatures could not occur.

Few zoos and no dealers are ready to supply information on the number of animals that have gone through their hands and on the time-span they were kept alive. Only where a "success story" may be told it has sometimes been written down. But even these are often disconcerting, like one of the renowned Krone Circus at Munich, Germany.

Krone has a combined group of Chimps and Orangs, kept to entertain people whilst having their meals round a table. They were treated with understanding and consideration by their keeper (who wrote the report), and were even given branches and leaves—a very rare privilege—to chew and build nests with. But the group was not too happy:

"Lore (a female Orang from Borneo—estimated 3-4 years old) is terribly frightened of the Chimps and is indeed treated badly by them. At the beginning, when the Chimps did not yet consider themselves the master of the cage, Lore felt reasonably secure. But later, when they had got used to the place and played their own games, they tried to make friends with the Orangs. With Buddha (a male from Sumatra, same age as Lore) it worked out all right, but Lore was uncooperative. She hid in a corner of the cage, all doubled up in anguish. If the two little black devils tried to approach her, she shrieked and her eyes protruded in fright. Eventually the Chimps teased her into such terror that she became completely stunned. As long as the others were about she did not dare move from her corner. When she remained there and I was in the cage to protect her she was left unmolested. But as soon as I turned my back and the Chimps saw me go away or if she moved unthinkingly, the Chimps jumped on her, scratched, kicked, bit her ; though seldom hard. Usually the attacks looked worse than they really were and probably no harm was meant. The Chimps just liked to show their power. Lore never defended herself. She crouched down, shrieking and crying . . ."[1]

Orangs, in contrast to Chimps, are not good entertainers at the so-called "tea-party" groups which have become a "must" in so many zoos and circuses. Their minds are not set to imitate, but to explore. Why is it that zoos and circuses insist on the idea of "teaching" them to sit on a chair or round a table? Would not a much greater crowd be drawn if they were let free in the trees of the zoo to show the spectators how they can move, climb, build nests ? The whole tea-party business is a ghastly, old-fashioned convention. And if it isn't, why not leave it to the Chimps to perform on their own ? They are capable of doing it without the help of tree-born Orangs or lonely Gorillas.[2]

[1] U. Prey, "Beobachtungen an den Orangs des Zirkus Krone (München)." *Der Zoologische Garten*, XVII, 1-5, 1950.

[2] Hediger ("Psychology of Animals in Zoos and Circuses," London, 1955) says that "both play and training often give excellent oppor-

During the second month of our leave, Tom and I were on our way to Austria when our car broke down near Munich and we were able to pay a visit to Hellabrunn Zoo. Two things we were keen to see: the large Wattled Cassowary that Tom had brought up from a chick—a chick which had made the journey from Aru Islands to Borneo in the bag of our friend the late Admiral Sir Charles Lambe, then C.-in-C., Far East; and the Orang-utans.

The Cassowary was fine. It was a pleasure to see him. He wandered majestically in a large compound, among kangaroos. The tall casque on top of his head had grown further still. He looked happy and well. His splendid colour-picture featured in

---

tunities for brightening up the daily existence of the animals in the Zoo, making it more significant, and giving the animal the necessary amount of exercise and occupation."

This is true; but play and exercise should be devised in a way as to appeal to the animal's way of thinking and inclinations; not to that of his "trainer."

It is important in this connection, to refer to an innovation at London Zoo, the "Chimpanzee-Den." Dr. Morris introduces this in The International Zoo Yearbook, *I*, 1959:

> "For many years the Chimpanzee tea-party on the central lawn has been a popular feature . . . but its appeal has always been *frankly anthropomorphic* and it can have done little to illuminate the true personality of the Chimpanzee. To do this it is necessary . . . to provide a more serious demonstration of their most impressive characteristic, namely their strikingly high degree of intelligence."

Dr. Morris goes on to describe all sorts of tests the Chimpanzees undergo in the new den: aiming with a ball, weight-lifting, and manipulating a "chimpomat" slot machine. The apes are given coins to obtain food from it.

> "The machine is similar to a human-operated slot machine, except that it has a side lever to be pulled down to open the reward draw. The drawer then shuts automatically . . ."

If this is not "frankly anthropomorphic" (though strikingly up-to-date) I don't know what is!

pride of place on the cover of Munich's Zoo-guide, which inside describes its ape-house as follows :

"Here live the breeding pairs and families of apes. The large playing compound outside, the covered gym-hall for bad weather and the large inner cages with sleeping-boxes at the sides are for the growing youngsters. This complex ape-house, which was built in 1936 cost a lot of money but was completely destroyed during the war. Its reconstruction was only gradually possible after the currency reform . . .

What surprises every visitor about the apes is to see how they slowly develop from intelligent, gentle children full of fun into *jungle-devils* that become dangerous charges owing to their excitable characters and strength, coupled with a formidable dentition, though they tend to love their keepers. Happily, a number of Chimpanzees and Orang-utans have been born at the Hellabrunn ape-house and there are Chimps living there in the third generation."[1]

This sounded all right (though one might question the "jungle-devils") and so it was as far as the Chimps went. They were playing in and outside, had learned many tricks and acrobatics (? ex Circus-Krone) which spectators enjoyed. They were walking ropes, jumping into the keeper's arms, sitting round a table, nicely mannered. They were humorous, relaxed and zoo-happy. But the Orangs were utterly "dull" from the spectator's point of view ; to me they looked deeply unhappy and frustrated. There were two of them, both half-grown—perhaps born in the zoo ? Their cage had a concrete floor and sloping shelves to climb on to, round the sides ; a low wooden table and chairs, where they sat—the keeper with them—oblivious of what they were supposed to do. They had grown out of cute babyhood and were at an age when they should have exercised their bodies over long hours to become strong and vigorous animals. When they

[1] H. Heck, "Führer durch den Tierpark Hellabrunn," Munich, 1960.

should have climbed, swung, investigated, built nests. Their hair was sparse and worn.

Most modern zoos forbid feeding by visitors, either absolutely or partially—and for good reasons. Much harm has been done to the animals, and especially to apes. Casualties were common but mostly hushed-up. Here is a typical example from San Diego, where a young Orang died in 1928, after less than a year in the zoo :

"Jiggs became more and more childlike as he grew weaker ; there was little left of him except the distended abdomen and the clinging fingers. He whimpered imploringly to each of us and, although we could do nothing for him, he loved to have us hold him in our arms. When one morning Henry came to tell me he was gone, I felt relief that his suffering was over. *Autopsy revealed that he had a big wad of gum, paper and all, in his stomach.* How he obtained it under Henry's watchful eye, we never knew. He could not rid himself of it as an older, stronger ape might have done. . . ."[1]

The common ill-effect of feeding by zoo visitors is, of course, that the animals eat much too much, become unnaturally fat, and inactive in consequence. An example was the adult Sumatran male who was acquired by the London Zoo in 1948 and lived there till his death in 1961. As well as pronounced and pendulous cheek callosities framing his face, he had a high hump of fat and flesh on top of his head and an ample fat reserve all over his body. He spent most of the last years lying hidden away in a bunch of straw. Only aroused when the keeper came near to call him or if he happened to glimpse a tempting bit of food thrown in, he would probably have not been able to move to an upper shelf even had there been one. Orangs like this would certainly be unfit to live in the jungle. Although fully mature, he was not able to produce offspring.

[1] Belle J. Benchley, *My Friends the Apes*, London, 1944.

It is possible, of course, that such inactivity is based on other serious disease as well. His predecessor, Sandy, for instance, lived in London Zoo for nineteen years—up to the age of about twenty-five. Professor Brandes writes of him:

". . . Unfortunately I was unable to find out at what age he developed his cheek callosities. Like the Dresden Orang, Peter, he was unable to stand on his legs; both of them could only crouch and slither forward. Sandy's rickets were worse than Peter's: his skeleton could not be preserved, as I found out at Tring, where his corpse had been sold. Even his skull crumbled away. In both cases it was possible to keep the animals alive for a long time, but it was the mere vegetation of two cripples; healthy adult animals were not brought up."[1]

Standards of food have of course improved since these early days, especially with regular doses of vitamins given to the animals in most zoos now.

The best type of ape food seems to be a combined diet of fruit and vegetables with a "Zoo-cake" compact food.[2] In addition fresh branches should be given—carefully if they have not been available for some time (as in winter): the animals tend to get into digestive trouble once they have been off branches for a period. This experience led some zoos to believe that branches and leaves were no good. It is perhaps possible that the trees in temperate zones contain some substance alien to an Orang and that a diet without greens is so detrimental to him that a few months' interruption can upset his system very badly.

No research has been done on the subject. Yet it seems that the most common causes of death in captivity, after eliminating pneumonia and related diseases, are a variety of pathological

[1] G. Brandes, "Der Tod unseres Riesenorangs 'Goliath,'" *Der Zoologische Garten*, I, 1929.

[2] A variety is described by F. A. Ulmer in "Breeding of Orang-utans," *Der Zoologische Garten*, XXIII, 1-3, 1957.

conditions of the stomach and intestines. These conditions may arise after short months, or long years, of captivity.

There is no doubt that Orangs *need* trees to grow up into healthy animals, to reach maturity and be capable of breeding. But it must be borne in mind that their whole system is so delicately balanced that any diet that takes them away from their natural way of life, including use of alien trees, must be given with caution.

The day is of course dull for the animals if visitors do *not* feed them. Stupor becomes overpowering if apes are kept without a companion or interest of any kind. But even a companion is not much fun in an empty cage with nothing to play at. The only possible occupation, then, is to observe the visitors. They are always intrigued by the appearance and behaviour of humans. But this alone cannot keep them healthy and happy for weeks and years.

An interesing comparison is the treatment of her children by an ill-witted Canadian mother. I quote from the *Daily Express*, 30th July, 1960:

HIDDEN 11 YEARS—WITH TV SET

Out into the sunlight after 11 years of darkness walked three children yesterday—frail, sunken-eyed, and tiny for their years. Their mother had kept them hidden in an upstairs room.

At first it was because she could not find a landlord who would take more than three children. And 45-year-old twice-married Mrs. Shirley Leach had six . . .

[After some years] she feared they would be *ridiculed for being so small* if they went to school. *None had been able to walk until they were eight.*

So they stayed indoors with their toys and a TV set. Their world was the view from an upstairs window—some trees, a garage, and a well-remembered rusty bicycle . . .

Yesterday little Gordon—14 years old but only 47 inches tall—walked out while his mother was at the dentist. . . .

Such is the effect of prolonged captivity and a life without exercise. Similar it must be for our friends, the apes, in zoos—though they, poor souls, cannot hope to "walk out" on us successfully.

Unhappily there is one ready excuse for not giving facilities for exercise and play ; especially not to Orangs. They have one ability which distinguishes them from the other apes : they take everything to pieces, an attitude also referred to as their "engineering skill." Bob behaved as a true representative of his kind when he made his début at San Diego. There are countless other examples of Orangs breaking out of cages and sleeping quarters by patient fiddling with strong fingers on locks and bars. Similarly, equipment is destroyed systematically by biting and tearing. A swinging rope strung up in a cage may be bitten away within a day. Textile covers, even sacks, are torn, wooden shelves and beams gnawed and bitten away. The more Orangs are encouraged by kind keepers who give and replace things, the more ingenious they get in destroying them again. After some time everybody—directors as well as keepers—give up ; the cages become bare. No more ropes, except perhaps a short strong bit of plastic or an iron chain ; no sacks ; one huge strong beam instead of a series ; one polished shelf (harder to tackle) instead of a rough one ; and a metal swing, if any. But this type of everlasting equipment is of no abiding interest to the curious Orang. Once tested and explored, moving about in it becomes a matter of routine—like the endless walk-abouts of a tiger behind the iron bars of his cage.

Thus the animals are punished for an attitude which is fundamental and necessary for their well-being in the jungle. They become "corrupted" and, if still young and growing, their development is arrested by the lack of incentive to exercise. Unless a lot more trouble is taken in the daily care of the animals, such as varying the equipment or toys in the cages at short intervals, or giving them regular exercise *outside* the cages, mortality rates will remain high.

2

In his book *The London Zoo*,[1] Mr. Philip Street has the following remarks about the breeding of apes in zoos :

> "So far apes have shown little inclination to breed in captivity. No gorilla birth has ever been reported, which is perhaps not surprising since so few have ever survived beyond maturity and these have mostly been solitary individuals. There are a few records of Orangs breeding, and in 1942 Edinburgh Zoo achieved the distinction of producing the first birth in a British zoo. Unfortunately, the infant lived for only three days."

In actual fact, there are a good many records of Orangs breeding—in those American and Continental zoos where the apes are properly cared for—and the British record is anything but distinguished. The first birth here was indeed in 1942—after Orangs had been kept in British zoos since 1837 without any of them producing offspring. However, in 1961 a baby was born to a pair of Sumatran Orangs which had been reared from infancy in London zoo. The first zoo baby was recorded in 1928 in Berlin, followed very closely by two others during that same year, in Nürnberg and Philadelphia. All three died in infancy because their mothers' milk was inadequate. They had not been correctly fed during pregnancy, and as a result their babies developed rickets during the first few months. But diets and standards of care improved from year to year. Further breeding followed, in Düsseldorf, Moscow, Dresden, Rome, St. Louis and Havana. Often the babies were removed from their mothers at the first signs of malnutrition, and brought up on the bottle. In Philadelphia, progress was outstanding indeed[2] : twelve

[1] 1956.
[2] Information is given by F. A. Ulmer, Jun. "Breeding of Orang-utans," *Der Zoologische Garten*, XXIII, 1-3, 1957.

babies were born between 1928 and 1953—three from a Bornean
pair, Chief Utan and Maggie, seven from a Sumatran pair, Guas
and Guarina, and two incestuously from Guas and his grown-up
daughter Ivy—the first record of a second generation bred in a
zoo. The succession of infants was as follows :

	YEAR BORN	SEX	NAME	REMARKS

Parents : "Chief Utan" x "Maggie" (Bornean)

	YEAR BORN	SEX	NAME	REMARKS
1	1928	m.	Lucky	Lived one year, died of malnutrition.
2	1930	m.	Norsuto	Lived 13 years, died by accident.
3	1932	?	premature birth	*Mother "Maggie" dies after birth.*

Parents : "Guas" x "Guarina" (Sumatran)

4	1935	f.	Cinderella	Reared by hand—exchanged to another zoo in 1944 where she died after contracting tuberculosis.
5	1937	f.	Ivy	Reared by hand, lives.
6	1940	m.	Rusty	Reared by hand, lives.
7	1943	f.	?	Died of rickets at 13 months—(mother refused to give it up).
8	1946	f.	Blondy	Stayed with mother for 13 months ; no signs of rickets, lives.
9	1949	m.	Pinkie	Stayed with mother for over a year, well nourished when separated, lives.
10	1952	m.	Lucky II	Looked after by mother but also given additional food, lives.

Parents : "Guas" x "Ivy" (cf. No. 5 above)

11	1950	f.	?	*Mother refused to care, due to youth and inexperience.* Baby died at two months, due to accidental overheating of incubator.

| 12 | 1953 | m. | ? | Mother cares, but due to overcrowding was not separated from her younger brother "Rusty." He bit the baby's hand, which caused its death at the age of ten days. |

The history of the Sumatran female called Guarina, is particularly informative. Prior to living at Philadelphia, she had been looked after at Havana, Cuba, where she had had her first offspring in 1929. Assuming that she was then approximately ten years of age, she had borne her last baby at the age of about thirty-three. The total number of her babies born was thus at least eight, six of which survived.

It may be assumed, then, that a healthy female normally remains fertile for as long as twenty-three to twenty-five years. And that, under *optimum zoo conditions*, she may have a baby every third year or so, provided the growing infant is taken away from her shortly after completing its first year. But there are many snags to this theory.

First, there are ample records of miscarriages, premature and difficult births. The first British birth record, in 1942 in Edinburgh, is an example. Here the mother was unable to feed the infant and refused to give it up to be reared by hand, resulting in its death within a week. She became pregnant again and died during birth of the second baby. She, like her mate, Mickey, came from Sumatra. Mickey was then introduced to a second mate, Mary, resulting in a further birth in 1952—as the director, Dr. G. D. Fisher, states, this and the former birth were "unexpected"—when the young one was killed by Mickey before he could be separated.

This is a danger common at zoos : conditions of overcrowding. When Guarina gave birth to her seventh baby, Pinky, her mate Guas was allowed to remain with her during the entire pregnancy and birth. The birth excited Guas sexually and he attempted to copulate with Guarina, who tried to avoid him. In the ensuing scuffle the baby was treated very roughly and the father had to be removed. However, the baby survived the ordeal. Later on, when Ivy gave birth to a male baby whilst sharing a cage with her younger brother Rusty. It was he who bit the baby in the hand. Ivy refused to give the infant up for treatment, and the resulting infection caused its death.

Two recent cases of difficult births (1960) come from Frankfurt and Vienna Zoos, where babies had to be removed by Caesarian operation; both mothers died subsequently. Dr. Spindler wrote me on this from Vienna:

"The (Vienna) mother died exactly three weeks after the operation—naturally from a sepsis. I am personally convinced that such a serious operation, in the case of apes, should be performed under the same clinical conditions and precautions that are taken for humans, in an operational theatre. It is not good enough to use a place where pigs, cattle, horses, etc., are operated on. Officially, of course, veterinaries do not want to agree with this view. . . ."

Though normally the birth itself is quickly over—the time span from the beginning of labour to delivery is approximately 8-10 minutes—inexperienced mothers often refuse, or are unable to care for and perform the necessary after-birth "rituals" in the proper way. An example of this attitude is the Orang mother Cleo at Berlin Zoo, who later had a terrible death during an air-raid in November, 1943 (as we shall see). She

"gave the impression that she was sick herself after the loss of her first husband, Hassan, who died in 1927 of tuberculosis. She was, by the way, a bad mother. The baby, born to her on 12.1.28, soon died as a result of her neglect. She often simply dropped it and seems to have taken very little interest in it. I cannot say whether the death of her husband had something to do with this attitude."[1]

Nowadays it is sometimes possible to bring up such babies by

[1] Graf Zedwitz: "Beobachtungen im Zoologischen Garten, Berlin," *Der Zoologische Garten*, Vol. II, pp. 283-285.

hand, as is being attempted, so far successfully, both in Frankfurt and Vienna.

Pre-war records at Berlin Zoo showed success on the breeding side, but failure in bringing up infants successfully. Cleo gave birth to five offspring. They were:

	SEX	DATE BORN	DIED
1.	fem.	12.1.28	14.2.28
2.	male	5.5.30	16.1.33
3.	male	13.1.34	7.6.35
4.	male	23.4.36	Given in 1938 to Munich's new ape-station, where it died soon after an accident.
5.	fem.	1939	Transferred to Copenhagen because of air-raids; it died there soon after the war.

Fortunately, standards of infant care have improved considerably since that time and it seems comparatively easy, these days, to bring up an Orang by hand—although this type of upbringing is no ideal substitute for mother's milk and education. Two factors are important: that the infant naturally relies on mother's milk for a long period—probably at least four years; and that the mother introduces the infant to masticated fruits, chewing of leaves and branches, as well as to exercise, at an early age. The growth rate of an infant brought up by mother in this way is slightly arrested compared to that of a bottle-fed baby. But its body becomes stronger and healthier.

Buschi, born in 1927 in the Red Sea while in transit to Europe, was brought up in Dresden Zoo. His mother's breast seemed very small at first and it was argued whether to take the baby away to rear it by hand. Fortunately this was not done, and both mother and infant developed splendidly. There were no signs of rickets or malnutrition—probably due to the fact that Professor Brandes was the first zoo director to insist that fresh branches and leaves were provided to the animals every day.

Suma breast-fed her offspring *over six and a half years* (though, of course, Buschi fed on fruit as well). No interruption of lactation was observed. However, shortly before the baby's fifth birthday, Suma was often seen pressing her breast against the bark of a living tree in her cage, thus taking milk from it. Buschi, observing this, used to catch the trickle with widely protruding lower lip— a sure sign (to me) that he was less hungry for this type of food. Suckling had become a game rather than necessity.[1]

It seems that more often than not babies have been deliberately removed from their mothers so that these could return to the males for further breeding. Rotterdam Zoo, for instance, have been most successful post-war in breeding Orangs from two males (Bonzo and Adriaan) and two females (Tineke and Julia), all imported fully grown from Sumatra. They produced six off-spring—four males, two females—and only one of them died in infancy. Dr. van Bemmel writes in a personal letter (22nd December, 1960):

> "All babies stayed with their mother till the age of one to one and a half years. In our experience the baby stops growing at that age, the lactation period seems at an end and a sort of food competition arises. It was impossible to make any weight statistics. The mother never will give any opportunity to take away the baby and a lot of trouble starts if the baby has to be separated from the mother at an age of one year or more."

It is perhaps reasonable to assess an approximate lactation period of four years in the wild state—gradually decreasing, with the youngster taking other food as well, from the age of roughly one year. At the age of four, an Orang is well on his way towards independence and strong enough, especially within a teen-age group, to defend and fend for himself. The period recorded at

[1] G. Brandes, "Die Stillzeit des Orang," *Der Zoologische Garten*, x, 3-4, 1938-9.

Bad zoo conditions. *Right*, concrete floors give no grip for the feet and graze the hair away; feeding by visitors is a cause of disease. *Below*, in Hamburg Zoo where Nigel and Frank found a home.

Füttern strengstens verboten!
Feeding strictly prohibited!

In good zoos Orangs can live and breed. *Left*, a mother and her baby at Frankfurt. *Below*, Mickey, the Sumatran Orang who died of old age in Edinburgh zoo

Dresden Zoo may have been artificially prolonged by confinement and lack of "group life." If a lactation period of approximately four years is assumed as a *natural* pattern for female Orangs living in the wild, we may conclude that one female, provided she remains healthy, may bear four to five offspring during her lifetime. Bearing in mind a possible infant mortality of forty per cent in the wild, an average two-three babies per female may be assessed.

Unfortunately, there is little information on the question why, in so many zoos, breeding has never been achieved. The bad cage facilities and care provided have already been suggested as one reason. Another (as for instance in New York Zoo) is the extreme obesity of males.[1] Apart from that it is interesting to note that zoos where breeding *was* achieved were sometimes unsuccessful in mating certain individuals. Orangs seem to select their sexual partner with consideration. An Orang may be quite happy to love the cage partner platonically if he or she does not meet the other's sexual requirements adequately.

An example is the female Julchen, imported from Sumatra in 1926 to Düsseldorf Zoo. A first male, Wambo, reached the same zoo in 1927. He developed the broad cheek callosities of complete manhood during the same year. Julchen and Wambo were brought together, but *Wambo took no notice of the female*, though she was already sexually mature (i.e. menstruating regularly).

In April, 1930, another male, Mawas, was imported and put together with Julchen, who was just menstruating. Both took a keen interest in each other at once.

"However there was no copulation during the days of the menstruations in May, June and July. The interval between

[1] Dr. L. S. Crandall writes in Dec., 1960, about their very large and obese male who has been living, since infancy, with a female.
"Copulation is attempted practically daily but there has been no pregnancy, quite possibly because the obesity of the male prevents successful intromission."

the first days of two successive menstruation periods was regularly thirty-two days; the dates being 26th May, 27th June, 29th July and 30th August. Only after the menstruation of the 30th August did copulation ensue—on 6th September, with repetitions on the 8th, 9th, 17th, 19th and 21st September. On 30th September another menstruation took place (again thirty-two days), with copulation following on the 1st and 2nd October. Further copulations were not observed. There was no menstruation in October, November and December, and on the 9th January, 1931, a miscarriage took place which unfortunately was not recovered because Julchen quickly ate the fœtus before the keeper could get hold of it. After the miscarriage the animals were separated for five days; on being reunited they promptly copulated on 15th and 16th January. Menstruation ceased from that time and no further copulation was observed. During the seventh month of pregnancy male and female were separated, and on the 18th October, 1931, a female baby was born and called Maja. Gestation period was 275 days."[1]

Thus, even with "keen interest," it took four months to the first copulation. It is also interesting to note that copulation ceased as soon as the female became pregnant. Unfortunately there is no published confirmation, from other zoos, of this attitude but Dr. van Bemmel wrote from Rotterdam recently:

"Bonzo had no other wife than Tineke. Adriaan prefers Tineke, but lives quite happily with Julia also. He cannot be kept with both females at one time.

"We put Adriaan several times together with another female, Jet (imported 1950). Jet came here together with her male baby, and must therefore be fertile. Adriaa mated several times with her, *apparently more or less against her will, without any results. Copulation ceases after the female has become pregnant.*"

[1] G. Aulmann, "Geglückte Nachzucht eines Orang-utan im Düsseldorfer Zoo," *Der Zoologische Garten*, v, 4-6, p. 83-90, 1932.

Copulation itself was observed in several instances and described by the late Professor Brandes thus :

"Suma did not experience successful copulation as long as she was with us. Goliath tried to rape her a few weeks after her arrival, when she was still carrying Buschi. He chased her amongst the branches of the cage, even got hold of her. But he had to release her again.

"Such rape on the part of the male may even result in *immissio* as it was the case in Berlin with Adam and Cleo and also later with Buschi. He was given a female companion that had lived for six months in a cage adjoining his. She was a scrappy, oldish animal called Meja and took flight at his violent approach. He soon caught her and raped her in the hanging position. The first ejaculation took place prior to *immissio* (the long, compact gelatinous cone dropped). The second attempt was successful and in the same abnormal position. It was never again adopted though copulations took place daily until February, 1938. At least nobody observed it.

"Mating is different if the female is willing. Not *more canum* (*a tergo*) as previously suggested for all apes. A loving Orang pair behaves in a peculiar way, as I have been able to see in two cases : in Frankfurt and at Cros des Cagnes. The same was observed by Fox in Philadelphia and Aulmann in Düsseldorf Zoo. The female lies down on her back—sometimes animated to do so by nudging. The male seizes with right and left (hands) the thighs of the female above her knees and pulls her body towards him as if it were a sack. He sits bending his torso backwards (thus half lying), spreads his thighs, knees bent. He holds the lips of her vulva open with his big toes and accomplishes *immissio*. In the one case the male nearly lay on his back during the coitus, only supported himself slightly upright by hanging from a branch with one hand. Here I saw how the female, who had borne all this patiently without apparent excitement, got up from the described position and bent over to the male so that her head came to rest on his thighs. This impressed me as a loving gesture. I was unable otherwise, as was Fox, to see signs of tenderness, and the animals were silent.

"It is easy to understand variations of this type of coitus when the partners squat facing each other as may be the case when there is little room, as for instance in trees. I saw Suma and Buschi (mother and son)—before Meja's arrival—sometimes in this position. But I was unable to observe coitus. . . .

"In this connection I should like to refer to the question whether an Orang possesses a *natural sense of shame*? Blyth asserts it for an adult female Orang he observed in Calcutta. The animal was supposed to have repeatedly tried to cover her genitals with a piece of plank, a bunch of straw or her own foot. I have never seen this myself and it is possible that such behaviour is based on *training* or that it was purely accidental. . . ."[1]

I should like to interpret the above Calcutta observation as masturbation, rather than training. As for the "sense of shame," is it not a purely human convention? Why should Orangs have it? Why should they worry about "covering their genitals" when there was never any need to do so? Orangs like to cover their *heads* if anything. But as there is no ready interpretation of this attitude, it has never been explained satisfactorily. It is remarkable that even Brandes, the first true friend of the caged Orang, falls into these homocentric absurdities.

An interesting feature of mating is the so-called "singing" of the males. It has been said to come from the Orangs' sleeping places by travellers and trappers; and the sound helped them to find the Orangs' nests. I have never heard it in that way myself, but Gaun told me he did. It is a low vibrating growl which gradually increases in intensity, like the sound of a motor-cycle approaching from a distance. It gains in vibrato until it becomes

[1] G. Brandes, "Buschi," Leipzig, 1939.

a deep roar, and then decreases again. The singing may last up to four minutes and several males may join in a contest : Brandes heard it at Cros de Cagnes where a new transport of Orang families had just arrived from Sumatra :

"An old male sang as our Goliath used to do and presently two others who sat opposite joined in. One is inclined to believe that this is their way to express their strength and to animate each other—in the wild, of course, and over long distances. Because Orang families will not dwell in the jungle as near each other as they were here. I cannot agree that the singing might be an expression of their longing (for instance for dead members of a family group) as had been suggested from Budapest. I saw one young male who had not yet got his broad cheeks copulate with a female with whom he shared a cage, soon after the singing."[1]

The fighting of males for a female has never been observed in the jungle. But there are indications that this happens. Many of the adult males imported in the thirties had injuries such as a torn nose septum, deep cuts and bruises on cheeks and necks, a finger bitten off, scars on arms and upper lip. It is possible, of course, that some of the injuries were caused during trapping ; but none of the females had thus been injured.

Again, Brandes describes a delightful aspect of family life observed at Dresden Zoo :

"If a male, let us say the head of the family, feeds, the female sits down near him and counts, so to speak, every bit into his mouth. This behaviour is so distinct that spectators often expressed their resentment at the selfishness of the male ! But I came to the conclusion that the female was neither jealous nor greedy for his food. If I approached her in such situations with special tit-bits, grapes for instance—even putting these right between her lips—she refused to accept them. It was

[1] op. cit.

her 'duty' to attend to the male first. Only after he completed his meal did she think of her own food."

There are numerous peoples in the world who have, or had, similar eating habits. I do not think that the female thus degrades herself. It seems a convenient and respectable way both to care for and control the male, and gives him a feeling of superiority at the same time !

The question remains open whether this is a universal habit with Orang ladies. Few zoos have taken the trouble to observe their animals regularly and publish results. If only they had, we might have a complete picture of the behaviour of our nearest relatives—at least, in captivity, where so many have suffered and died to delight millions of civilised humans.

3

". . . On the next expedition to the Orient *he made a supreme effort to obtain an exhibit similar to one of the family groups that had been collected* by the firm of Louis Ruhe of Hanover, in 1927. These adult pairs, most of whom were accompanied by babies or juveniles, constituted the most extraordinary collection of apes ever brought from any jungle. The collection, I understand, consisted of twenty-seven[1] specimens, including perhaps eight mated pairs. It was the first time that adult giant male Orangs had ever been brought alive into zoos. The final outcome, however, was a tragedy. Few, if any, lived long enough to bring another young one into the world, and little actual scientific work was done while they remained alive. Published reports have dwelt at some length upon the remarkable diversity in the Orang's appearance, the different shapes and sizes of the cheek callosities,[2] the length and patterns among the beards and other hirsute adornment. If the individuals in the collection just mentioned had been

[1] There were in fact thirty-three.   [2] A feature of adult Orangs.

more scientifically observed while in captivity and if a proper recording of their activities in the wild had been brought back with them, a much longer life and more valuable information would almost surely have been the reward. It is doubtful if such a collection will ever again be made, for the Orang has already disappeared from many of his former territorial limits, and is now confined almost exclusively to Sumatra and Borneo."[1]

Mrs. Benchley, a former Director of San Diego Zoo, refers here to the second Ruhe shipment sold in 1927 *in toto* to Ringling in the U.S. (see p. 145). Apparently thirty-one animals reached their final destination alive. I have been unable to follow up any one individual of that particular shipment: neither of the two breeding pairs at Philadelphia originally belonged to the group. It would have helped matters tremendously if any of the zoos concerned had observed these animals regularly and published such work. I don't, however, agree with Mrs. Benchley, that the trapping of another group of Orangs could ever be the remedy to the situation. Orangs are, and, in historic times, always have been confined *exclusively* to Sumatra and Borneo and are threatened with extinction within a decade or little more. If large numbers, and breeding pairs are taken away from their last refuges *before* facilities and knowledge in zoos generally improves, the result can only be disastrous.

Scientific observations on Orangs have been carried out by a very few zoos—the significant portions of which I have already incorporated in this story. Unfortunately much of this work was destroyed as a result of the Second World War. It is now up to those fortunate enough to house Orangs capable of breeding—to carry on that work and to bring up animals in zoos that will be capable of breeding a second and third generation.

It is comparatively easy to start off with a healthy baby, better with two, if the standards of care are high and a devoted person looks after them as at Edinburgh Zoo, where I went to see Ossy

[1] Belle J. Benchley, *My Friends, the Apes*, London, 1944.

and Derek later in the summer of 1960. Over two months had passed since I had last covered their cage in the animal hospital at Regent's Park with a blanket, so that they should not be aware of my going. I was keen to see how they had settled in, so flew up from London for the week-end.

It was a miserable Sunday. The two little faces peeped through the large glass wall of their "sun-porch" into fog and rain. There were shelves to sit high, if required; a climbing construction and ropes to grip. The floor was littered with toys. When I got near they both crowded on the inner side of the glass, in quick recognition. They looked well and grown. Their hair was long and shiny as it used to be. Presently Mrs. Macpherson came to give them their bottle. She took me inside to greet them properly. I was not surprised that they clung to her (Derek more so than Ossy) and very nearly disregarded me. They had adopted her completely and so it should be. They needed a mother and had found a very good one, for Mrs. Macpherson was devoted to them. Nobody else in the world mattered, not even ex-mother.

The next step—to lead a growing baby from the toddler stage into adolescence—is a much harder one to take in a zoo. For this is the time when the young Orang should be taught to move, to exercise his body. He will only do it, though, if you give him something to arouse his curiosity, if he has an incentive and proper facilities. Tables, chairs and "tea-party" manners are of no interest to him whatever, and you cannot really teach him football or other such exacting games.

Well, the Orangs themselves have demonstrated simply what can be done. Here are two examples of what I mean. The first one from London:

"The nest-building instinct must be very firmly fixed, judging from an incident that took place at Regent's Park some time ago. Jacob, a large male Orang, succeeded one night in breaking out of his cage into the Monkey House, and from there through a skylight on to the roof, eventually finding his way into a tall overhanging tree. By the time his escape was discovered early the following morning, Jacob was already curled up in a nest that he had made among the topmost branches. The interesting feature about this escapade is that he had been living at the Zoo for many years, during which time he had neither built nor seen a tree nest, yet when the opportunity arose the urge and ability to construct one were both available."[1]

I should have said the urge and need were paramount. This Orang demonstrated, wildly enough, how he wanted to live. Then *why not build him an enclosure round a tree*? And if this is impossible, and I see no reason why it should be, why not give him at least some large branches to construct a nest within his cage?

The approach at San Diego was more sympathetic. Here a young female Orang behaved in the same way when Mrs. Benchley "coaxed the keeper, Henry, to release the Orang's hand near a young but sturdy black acacia tree. She needed no hint . . ." She climbed up and made herself a perfect nest in the tree. Nobody had shown or demonstrated to her what to do. She did it—and left everybody spellbound. Mrs. Benchley concludes:

"This demonstration of mechanical ability was very wonderful to me at the time. I have since become convinced that it is *characteristic of Orangs and is not the mechanical genius of one or two specimens.* We have demonstrated it time after time with others young enough to be turned loose in the grounds."[2]

San Diego has developed this understanding attitude under new directorship. Growing youngsters are introduced to a "Primate Behaviour Laboratory," a combination exhibit cage with retiring and observation quarters. The present objects of study: two Orang-utans (our Bob and his mate Noëll, born in the zoo; two Chimpanzees and one Lowland Gorilla). Mrs.

[1] Philip Street, *The London Zoo*, London, 1956.
[2] Belle J. Benchley, *My Friends, the Apes*, London, 1944.

Rice, a graduate student of psychology describes[1] how Bob, on the first day, attempted to climb a tree but fell out and sat on the ground nursing his bruises. How he discovered endless play possibilities in a denuded eucalyptus tree and finally sat on the floor throwing leaves over his own head (this he had done as a baby in Pig Lane, using rice-grains or hay when the lawn had been cut). How he arranged twigs and branches laying them out parallel, in a neat pile. Mrs. Rice summarises his present personality thus :

"Bob's rather foolish, puzzled expression doesn't necessarily reflect his thoughts, if any, but upon at least one occasion it seemed singularly appropriate. Everywhere he went, he took with him one of the branches that had been removed from the eucalyptus tree. It was about eight feet long, perfectly straight, approximately an inch in diameter at the base, with a few leaves left on the tip. He carried it for a while, chewed on it pensively, then dragged it round and round the cage. Finally he sat down, studied his branch for a few moments, then raised it to an upright position. Holding it firmly perpendicular to the floor, he made a spectacular unsuccessful attempt to climb it—the ape version of the Indian rope trick !"

What is required for these growing youngsters are grounds with trees where they are left to do as they please, preferably with a number of teen-age playmates of their own kind. Ideally the grounds should be large with many trees in them. But a small area with only one tree is better than to leave the animals in the cage at all times. There is no need to fear that they will forget in the long winter months of a temperate climate what they can do in a tree !

The last month of our 1960 leave I spent in Germany. And as I

---

[1] Carol Rice, "First Day of School," *Zoonooz*, Nov., 1960, San Diego Zoological Society.

was worried about Nigel and Frank, confined to a cage after so
much freedom, I went to Hamburg first. Director Hagenbeck
had duly informed me of their début as follows :

"Yesterday afternoon the two Orangs were brought to Stellingen in cases we had brought along to the ship (the original
case fitted into the ship's hold so tightly that it could not be
removed) and they were immediately released into a larger
playing ground. The keeper had not quite left the cage when
both of them started a wild chase ; with their exacting play
they very nearly excelled the Chimpanzees ! I thank you
very much for these extremely healthy animals ; I have never
seen imported Orangs that were so well developed at so early
an age. This morning the two Orangs were visibly impressed
by their neighbours, a group of Chimps and Orangs which
they could see in a reflecting glass. Your two sat in a corner
and obviously did not want to be separated. . . ."

When I had managed to drive my car through traffic-con-
gested Hamburg into Stellingen, it was already late and the
zoo gates were about to be shut. I went straight to the ape-
house, where everybody had been put to bed. I explained who
I was and the kind keeper let me in, to say "hallo" to Nigel
and Frank in their sleeping boxes. As I extended my hands
through the bars they greeted me, and sat up to look at me
properly. For the first time I was frustrated by the inability to
talk to them. When they had been in my care and in constant
contact, it was easy to see what they wanted and there was
no need for talk. Now, I wanted to know if they were happy,
if they wanted to stay where they were ! The fact that they
were not in a frenzy about me and were lying down for sleep
whilst I was still there, reassured me. They were relaxed and
at ease in their new home. The past in tropical Borneo was
forgotten—or was it ?

Next morning, I was taken on a conducted tour of the park,
ending up at the ape-house. One of the roomy outside cages
held three Orangs. Frank, Nigel and a female of Nigel's size.

The female sat on an upper shelf, motionless. Nigel and Frank were on the move. They stopped when they saw me coming, but soon were off again to swing and climb. Mr. Hagenbeck told me that they were active at all hours of the day.

I begged him to give the animals green branches and leaves.

"Anything: oak, poplar, willow—whatever you can spare will do, as long as it is green and fresh."

There were plenty of trees in the park. Presently a large branch of oak was provided and all three Orangs grabbed for it. Each secured as much as possible and started a nest—including the female that had never seen or done it before. She did it right on the floor in a far corner of the cage; Nigel on a high shelf; Frank playfully here and there.

A large crowd assembled to see what they were doing. For once there were more spectators here than in front of the Chimps' cage next door. If only I could have opened their cage and let them free in the park!

4

My last stop-over before returning to Sarawak was in West Berlin. My mother gave me room in her flat there to sit down and write this story about Orangs. It was a matter of twenty minutes to drive into town and the zoo—which I had last seen in 1945, burnt out and wrecked. An air-raid in November, 1943, destroyed most of the grounds; but a large number of the animals were rescued. Lutz Heck tells of the events in the ape-house during that night:

"In that corner of the Gardens, in tropical heat (the coke heap burned incessantly for nearly a month outside the house), the Orang-utan Cleo[1] came to her end. The monkey-house had suffered a serious hit. A bomb had torn down the outer wall of one wing, where Cleo and the Chimpanzees Ova

[1] See p. 178.

and Bambu lived. They were now free. Other cages had been burst open by the shock, or glass panes had been smashed, and so many small monkeys also gained a freedom that had no attraction for them, for it led only into cold and rain and hunger.

"Cleo, already twenty years old, had given birth a year before to a young one that was living with her in the cage. Mother and child took refuge outside in a case, in which they passed the night of the bombing. Next morning Cleo let her child go back and wandered alone in the Gardens. She was a heavy animal, over twelve stone, and vicious ; Head-keeper Liebetreu said it would be impossible to capture her. Frau Liebetreu with the little one giving penetrating squeaks in her arms, followed the mother ; but the Orang-utan was not to be tempted ; she climbed high up a tree. She had to be left there for the time, and later, when it was possible to go back to her, she had disappeared. Search was made for four days ; then she was found by the burning coke heap—but she was dead. Probably she had been poisoned by the fumes, had lost consciousness and had succumbed to privation. . . ."[1]

The old ape-house was patched up and the remaining collections kept under difficult conditions for fifteen years. In 1955 two Orang-utans were again on show : two males imported from Indonesian Borneo, both just over a year old at that time. They developed well, but it is interesting to see the difference between them and the other three Orangs that were imported in early 1959 and put straight into the new ape-house. Two of them, a pair, were three years old at the time and came from Sumatra. The third, also three years old on arrival in late 1958, was our Eve. All three had retained their long shiny hair, whereas the two older Bornean Orangs had lost much of it during the time they had spent in the old ape-house.

[1] Lutz Heck, *Animals My Adventure*, Ullstein Verlag, Austria, 1952.

The new ape-house in Berlin is a marvellous affair. It has very large cages, in and outside, equipped with beams, shelves and swings as well as the conventional tables and chairs. The floor is very smooth—some sort of plastic—but when I went to see Eve and her companions, they had been put in an upstairs playing room, because they had managed to peel away some of it !

The Director, Dr. Klös, took me to see them.

"I wonder if you will recognise Eve," he said.

"I have no doubt that I will. Don't you think so ?"

"Well, Jenny and Jocky are just her size and colour, and it is nearly three years since you saw her last !"

We went into their room and all three crowded round us at the door. I picked Eve out without even thinking. She had grown, yes ; but somehow the expression on her face had remained the same—the others just looked quite different to me.

"I hoped you would recognise her," said Dr. Klös, "because I am of opinion that you can pick out and remember any one Orang once you have known him well—they all have their distinct expression and personality !"

She was in perfect condition with a pouch (but not too much) under her chin. She was not shy, quite at ease in my arms.

"Do you think she remembers you ?" He looked at me somewhat sceptically.

"I don't think so, because naturally she is *interested* if somebody comes to see her up here where there are no spectators. There may be something at the back of her mind ; I am fairly certain she would recognise Bidai, though."

Apart from the expression in face and personality, there was no difference at all between the Sumatran pair and our Bornean child. All three were of light, nearly golden red colour ; but then, Eve had always been the fairest of my children.

Dr. Klös showed me the facilities : a special ape-bathroom with a glass wall so that children may look in. A notice-board outside gives the particulars of whose turn it is at what time. An ape-kitchen where the meals are prepared. Best of all is the open playground, adjoining the young Orangs' cage. Here are no bars, but a large tree with various constructions for climbing round it. Eve and her companions are taken out during the whole summer—and with every bit of sunshine in winter.

"Do you see the oak-tree just in front of the ape-house, outside the compound ?" Dr. Klös pointed to a tall tree that was just shedding its leaves—it looked somewhat scrappy to me, but I was oblivious of what I was supposed to see.

"Don't you notice anything ? Look at half height and in the crown : don't you know what that is ?"

Of course ! How stupid of me ! there were *nests* in the tree ; nests made by Orangs !

He told me that often during the past summer he had taken them into the park, to let them climb the trees, during visiting hours. The public had been amazed to see the animals making themselves nests ! I was delighted too ; so it can be done !

"And do you know who was the only one who did *not* build nests ?"

I said that I didn't.

"Eve," he said, "your darling. She never tried yet. . . . I think she is too fond of Walter, her keeper."

CONCLUSION

Has the Orang a Future?

With Tom Harrisson

The technophobe animal—essentially the free wild animal—has basically two means of withdrawal from man's disturbing influences. It can change either its place or its time. In districts where they are greatly exposed to persecution, many diurnal animals become nocturnal, changing their times of activity. The other possibility is to give up the familiar space. This is no doubt the more drastic way of avoiding man with the least chances of success.

Prof. Dr. Heini Hediger,
Zürich, 1955

AT THE PRESENT MOMENT WE BELIEVE THAT THERE ARE far less than a thousand free Orangs in Sarawak. The information is somewhat obscure for our sister country of North Borneo but it seems doubtful if there are many more there, however loudly they shout !

There are none left in the State of Brunei, between North Borneo and Sarawak. Such meagre evidence as is now available from the large area of Indonesian Borneo territory indicates a continuing, almost uncontrolled exploitation of Orangs there—whatever intentions and regulations are in force on paper. The situation in Sumatra is still more serious and is accentuated by the presence there of soldiers with rifles, and by the proximity of the Asian mainland and the difficulty of controlling smugglers in sailing sampans.[1]

The situation in Indonesia, the largest area involved, is further complicated by the granting of private licences to own Orangs as "personal pets" to privileged people, who subsequently export them. There is no check on whether an export licence concerns the same animal as the one for which a pet licence was granted earlier.

[1] The local dealers' price for a baby Orang-utan is between £60 and £100. The only comparable form of animal contrabrand is rhinoceros horn. This the West no longer values, but is now exported to the East (even through antique dealers in the West End of London) for it is the No. 1 Chinese aphrodisiac. But the Two-horned Rhino of Borneo is already past this stage of smuggling ; there are only a few isolated animals left. Fifty years ago it was still numerous. Its final extermination is being brought about by the same sort of un-bridled cash-avarice as is tending, if slightly more slowly, to have the same effect on the Orang—and the other animals which attract either the sexual or the visual organs of non-Bornean women and men.

We think, though, that it is safe to put the world population of Orangs in 1961 as under 5,000. It may well be half this. It is probable that in the early centuries of the Christian era it was *at least* half a million. A thousand years ago there were still more apes than men in Borneo (to-day the island's few thousand Orangs match with about three million humans).[1]

What has been steadily happening, over a long period of time, is this : the steady restriction of the Orang into more and more limited areas, farther and farther away from expanding human populations and easy human access. With newly developing communications, particularly in North Borneo, this trend has been much accelerated in the past decade.

The remaining populations of Orangs are thus becoming increasingly vulnerable. Perhaps even more serious, they are becoming increasingly fragmented. Thus the Sarawak figure of well below 1,000 for a country of 48,000 square miles, is even more meagre than it may sound from a distance. There are no longer anywhere hundreds of Orangs in one area. They are all broken up into small parties ; and lately even individually. Further, human inroads are more and more cutting off group contact and interchange, continually restricting the "free roaming zones" which Orangs prefer (and probably need).

Political complications do not simplify this picture. Most of the remaining Orang populations in Sarawak territory are close to the Indonesian border, Kalimantan. One of the main Orang territories in North Borneo is on the Kinabatangan River, and is readily accessible from the northern end of Indonesian Borneo. There is little effective or possible control, along much of this jungle border.

Field information is awfully meagre. As we have already pointed out, the desire first to kill and then increasingly to capture Orangs seems somehow to have blinded zoologists of all kinds.

[1] North Borneo has 30,000 square miles, Indonesian Borneo 215,000 square miles ; compare England and Wales, 58,000 square miles.

HAS THE ORANG A FUTURE?

Apart from the observations of Sarawak Museum personnel in recent years, augmented by Dr. George Schaller working with us in the field for two months at the end of 1960, no one has seriously attempted to study the natural behaviour of wild Orangs. It is also (as we have seen in previous chapters), astonishing to observe to what extent zoological societies of status have failed to keep elementary records on Orangs in captivity. They have failed to fulfil a clear obligation (sometimes stated in the actual charters of foundation) to study precious and delicate animals so long confined in the name (partly) of science.

In attempting to assess, therefore, the *future* of Orangs, we must rely on our own inadequate Sarawak information. We believe, then, that probably less than one in five of wild Orangs living to-day are immature. And that an excessive proportion are old and even senile males, not infrequently living in isolation. These males are tough and long-lived ; and unless they become troublesome close to Durian orchards they are unlikely to attract the hostile or avaricious attention of anyone. There is a continuous selective human pressure on females with babies. The normal procedure is still to kill the female to get a baby.

The last zoo collector permitted to operate legally in Sarawak in 1946 removed fourteen or more young Orangs alive.[2] To achieve this, we know for certain that twenty others died as immediate consequence. At least twenty more were then killed because the Dayaks thought that everybody could now help themselves once again. In the following year, when T.H. became Curator of the Museum, no less than twelve illegally-acquired Orangs were confiscated and placed in his care as a result. Since then, not less than twenty more babies are known to have been through Sarawak hands in this way. It is only in the last five years that controls have been sufficiently effective to make it fairly sure that, for better or for worse, what comes into Sarawak from Indonesia must *all* end up in official charge.

In North Borneo, small but steady numbers have been

[2] He was accredited by the London Zoo, in writing.

exported officially. A characteristic item from the *Sunday Times* of 23rd August, 1959, runs :

"Singapore, Sat.—One-year-old Martha, an Orang-utan from the North Borneo wilds, was given the full VIP treatment when she arrived by Malayan Airways from Jesselton to-day.

"Martha, a gift from the North Borneo Government, is on her way to the Copenhagen Zoological Gardens, which is celebrating its 100th anniversary. A full meal was laid out for her at Singapore Airport and a new *suit of clothes* was ready for her to change into.

"But though Martha was ready enough to drink the two bottles of milk and eat the assorted fruits, she refused to wear the natty 'sailor suit' that had been made for her.

"In the end, she had her way and remained in her primitive natural state."

It would be hard to surpass the intellectual squalor of civilised man thus degrading a young woman of the jungle. But the welcoming committee in Singapore were evidently unaware of the risk they ran in thus handling a Bornean animal : the risk of everlasting and almost instantaneous damnation, through petrification. Over most of that Borneo to which poor Martha has said good-bye for ever, it is believed that even any *attempt* to dress up an animal in parody of humanity is the greatest of all human crimes, along with incest.

No export *statistics* are available from Indonesia, where we vaguely have to suppose—and hope—that a considerable number of Orangs do still survive. Many animal dealers are still maintaining direct contact with Indonesia. And there is no other way a *dealer* (as opposed to an accredited zoo) can acquire an Orang direct, except by the already described border-smuggling out of Sarawak and North Borneo through Indonesia.[1]

[1] Dr. Lee S. Crandall, New York Zoological Society, writes on this in December, 1960, in a personal letter :
"I have been attempting a check on the Orang-utans in captivity

HAS THE ORANG A FUTURE?

A handful of top-flight dealers can still obtain licences direct, however.   But recently the Indonesian Government has been refusing independent travellers permission to visit most parts of Indonesia territory, for reasons of their own safety.   However, as late as 1957 the Swiss Peter Ryhiner visited South Borneo after obtaining a permit in Java.   In his *The Wildest Game* (an apt description of his profession) Ryhiner has himself described what happened :

> "This time I went to Bogor (Java) and found the officials in the conservation department very reasonable and knowledge-able men.   They gave me a permit to capture two orangs, to be delivered only to the Colombo Zoo, and added, 'If, after getting your pair, you find any baby orangs in the native villages, buy them at once.   Don't worry about the permits . . . we'll issue them to you later.   The villagers can't keep the babies alive more than a few weeks.   The little apes pick up human diseases too easily, so they'd be lost anyhow.'   This was exactly what I'd found with young gorillas in Africa.   I thanked the men sincerely and, feeling much better about my chances in Indonesia, made plans for my trappings."

What, then, can be concluded on the smuggled out or licensed "in" ends of this sad chain, statistically ?

What does that mean in future *demand pressures* ? At present, the expectation of life of an Orang in an average zoo is three and

---

in this country for Harold Coolidge and find that the great majority arrived here in the 1950's, mostly from 1955 on.   These practically all came from dealers, so that their origin is only conjectural.   On that point you are aware, of course, that many young animals are—or have been—smuggled to Singapore from Borneo and perhaps Sumatra as well.   Once there, it is easy to circumvent a United States Customs regulation requiring an export certificate from the country of origin.   About 1950, the International Union of Directors of Zoological Gardens was active in seeking the co-operation of the authorities at Singapore in suppressing this traffic . . ."

a half years. It is much lower outside zoos and lower in some of the small "private" and provincial zoos. It is higher in the few zoos that treat Orangs as great apes rather than convicted rapists. In zoos like Philadelphia, San Diego, Rotterdam, an Orang, at this moment, may even have a better expectation of life than in the remaining wilds of Borneo or Sumatra.

If Orangs were given the same sort of priority treatment as lions, sea-lions or polar bears in most zoos, and if the experience of a few zoos where they have successfully matured, kept fit and bred was called upon, the future of the species might be insured in captivity. It will be an abject thing if the insatiable *Homo sapiens* can leave no corner of the world for the most amiable and unassuming of his cousins. Mankind is in a fair way to reducing the Orang (no doubt along with the Gorilla) to the same dependent status as that already the lot of the European Bison and Père David's Deer of China. But, abject or not, at least this way some Orangs would be sure of survival.

Orangs in zoos are numerous : 245 or more. But if the situation in the *wild* is as urgent and drastic as we have suggested, why so it soon will be in zoos too ! The present annual captive repro-duction rate of Orangs averages under five babies for the whole world. To keep up the *present* world zoo population (and zoo demands are rapidly increasing) would require sixty Orangs a year[1] being brought from Sumatra and Borneo. As this now has to be done largely at the native smuggling level, it is safe to estimate that for every one Orang brought out and sold to a dealer, three more have been killed : two mothers shot to obtain two babies—— with one of the babies dying before reaching reasonable standards of human care.

Even under ideal and legal conditions of pre-war controlled trading by experts, each Orang displayed in a zoo cost another life on the way. The loss was often much higher than that.

[1] Calculated on the basis of 240 zoo animals with an average long-evity of four years.

Under existing conditions and for the present estimate, let us then take a conservative minimum of *three dead for one alive* delivered in Edinburgh or Chicago, 1962. This means, simply, that to keep up the world population of captive Orangs for the next ten years will require this procedure :

> 60 fresh live Orangs per year :
> = 180 Orangs killed or dying in transit to produce 60 delivered
> = 240 a year
> = 240 × 10 = 2,400 in ten years

Not even on the most hopeful estimate can there be that many catchable Orangs left wild. It may be there are not even that many free Orangs of *all* ages and in *every* degree of isolation, anywhere.

The situation, if continuing unchecked, will clearly be disastrous. Yet it is difficult to see how it *can* be checked—on the negative, control side—when the price incentives are so high, the terrain so difficult, and the chief government involved has such mighty problems in its own territories that with the best will in the world it needs practically all its present resources to cope with immediate human matters of life and death.

Leaving aside pious hope and wishful thinking, it would seem that seven things *can* be done that *must* be done, now, at once, if the Orang is to survive into the next century :

1. The burden for export *control* must not be left simply to the countries which have wild Orangs—namely the Republic of Indonesia, Sarawak and North Borneo.

But it is not enough to have international conferences and organisations passing resolutions, as they regularly and properly do. Of themselves, such recommendations and resolutions achieve little ; and they sometimes have the effect of lulling those who have passed them into feeling that something real has been achieved in fact. No : the responsibilities here lie direct and clear upon zoos, too. Particularly upon the great zoological societies of international repute. They must set new standards and act together, without further delay, to restrict and outlaw illegal trading in Orangs.

2. *Much higher standards* must also be set for the care of apes in captivity, with *particular reference to breeding.* Standards should be agreed internationally and with the relative governments informed at a high level.

3. The zoos must exercise more *self-control and less selfishness* in acquiring ape exhibits, especially in acquiring "at all costs" for their own commercial reasons, single specimens of Orang (of course, this equally applies to other rare animals) which cannot possibly even be happy, let alone breed.

4. A specialist conference should be called to discuss measures to promote *breeding in captivity* and an international research foundation be set up with this immediate goal : the pooling of all information on breeding in captivity and the developing of further breeding and conservation techniques (in co-operation with responsible zoological societies).

5. That, as a corollary of the above, an international research project be sponsored to assist *the Indonesian and other governments*, both in ascertaining present Orang population accurately, and in devising practicable methods to preserve their status.

    (N.B. This has to be done without patronising or interfering with independent people, but as technical assistance —not coming from any one country or point of view ; and limited to this specific project.)

6. That dealings in protected animals (including the Orang) by private businessmen (i.e. animal dealers) be outlawed. Zoos and scientific institutions should acquire these animals

through a recognised international organisation on a non-profit basis.

In Sarawak, wide interest is already aroused.[1]

We believe that there is an opportunity in Sarawak:

7. To form at least one proper sanctuary for Orangs before it is too late; and to enlarge the scope and personnel of Orang research, with outside assistance, to study those other urgent problems which can only be seen *in the wild*.

The question really boils down to this: CAN WE BE IN TIME OR IS IT ALREADY TOO LATE?

The answer we are bound to find, for better or worse, in the too near future. At least, let some of us energetically seek to find it, whatever the research resources. Every field observation, apart from scientific value, in itself may assist materially in developing better ways of keeping Orangs in captivity and conserving them in the world. At the moment, whether we like it or not, we have to face the fact that it looks like somewhere near a forty-sixty chance of "the captive solution" being the only way to keep these great apes alive for our great grandchildren—at least.

This leaves one other fundamental question: Is it right to pay this price for keeping the Orang alive? Should they be in zoos at all? We like good zoos and have kept many Borneo animals as pets ourselves—many times as many as those mentioned in this book. But we feel that the Orang is a special case and needs human re-thinking. Is it too much to hope that our own private, simple, small-scale and inexpensive experiments in Pig Lane may not at least imply a way which could be followed up by the great, rich, public institutions of the world. A way to keep Orangs free, yet for view. . . .

[1] An independent advisory commission (consisting of Mr. D. L. Bruen and Dr. N. S. Haile) submitted recommendations for future protection of the Orang.

And if the worst comes to the worst, perhaps man can presently repay his load of evolutionary guilt by acquiring enough knowledge to *put back* a new generation of "western-born Orangs," to re-enter their Asian homeland afresh ?

It's a reflection on our time, though. No ? The other answer might, for instance, be taken to imply that a mankind which can find no living space for its cousin unchained is no longer fit to "control" the world, but has become a threat to the substance and meaning of life itself. At that stage, somewhere along the line, evolution passes on—past *Pongo pygmaeus* extinguished ; passing *Homo sapiens* the extinguisher ; to a new climax, more capable of balancing the universe's intricate equations (which cannot exclude tolerance and a check on specific indulgence of self).

APPENDICES

APPENDIX I:

DECIDUOUS AND PERMANENT DENTITION OF ORANG-UTAN

Upper Deciduous Dentition:

A = $6\frac{1}{2}$ months
B = $9\frac{1}{2}$ months
C = 11–12 months
D = $8\frac{1}{2}$–9 months
E = 10–$10\frac{1}{2}$ months

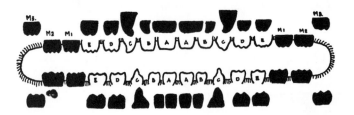

Lower Deciduous Dentition:

A = $4\frac{1}{2}$ months
B = $7\frac{1}{2}$ months
C = 11–12 months
D = 9–$9\frac{1}{2}$ months
E = 10–$10\frac{1}{2}$ months

First Permanent Molars M^1 = 4th year
Second Permanent Molars M^2 = 6th year
Third Permanent Molars M^3 = 12th–15th year

Permanent Dentition starting by the end of the fifth year

DENTITIONS OF ORANGS AND MAN

DECIDUOUS AND PERMANENT DENTITION OF HUMANS

Upper Deciduous Dentition:

A = 6 months
B = 7 months
C = 16 months
D = 12 months
E = 20 months

Lower Deciduous Dentition:

A = 6 months
B = 7 months
C = 17 months
D = 12 months
E = 20 months

First Permanent Molars M^1 = 6–7 years
Second Permanent Molars M^2 = 11–13 years
Third Permanent Molars M^3 = 17–21 years

Permanent Dentition starting by the sixth year

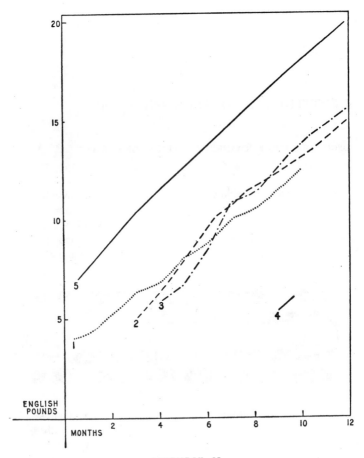

APPENDIX II

WEIGHT CURVES OF ORANG-UTAN BABIES

1 = ♀ ROBERTA, SAN DIEGO ZOO

2 = ♂ BOBBY, DUSSELDORF ZOO

3 = OSSY

4 = ♀ JANIE (DIED)

COMPARE:

5 = AVERAGE WEIGHT CURVE OF (ASIAN)
HUMAN BABIES

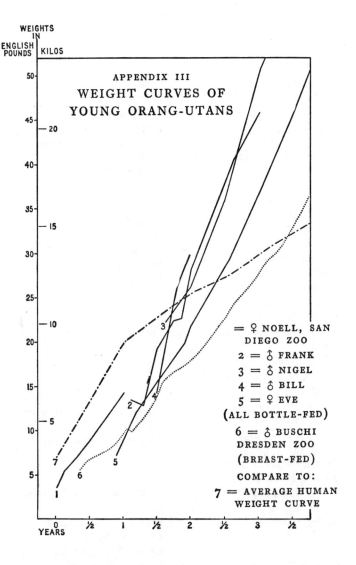

APPENDIX III

WEIGHT CURVES OF YOUNG ORANG-UTANS

= ♀ NOELL, SAN DIEGO ZOO

2 = ♂ FRANK

3 = ♂ NIGEL

4 = ♂ BILL

5 = ♀ EVE

(ALL BOTTLE-FED)

6 = ♂ BUSCHI DRESDEN ZOO (BREAST-FED)

COMPARE TO:

7 = AVERAGE HUMAN WEIGHT CURVE

INDEX

Abell, Sir Anthony, 45
Ali, Rajak, 20
Alloway, Mrs., 43
Angola, 12
Aru Islands, 169
Aulmann, Dr. G., 124, 127, 182-3

Bakar, 55, 63-4, 67
Balai Ringen Forest Reserve, 114
Banting, 21
Beccari, Count, 22
Beeckman, Capt. Daniel, 13-14
Belawan, 142, 147
van Bemmel, Dr., 180, 182
Benchley, Belle J., 171, 187, 189
van den Bergh, Dr., 113
Bidai, 34-8, 41, 46-7, 49, 91, 117, 129
Bontius, Jacob, 12-14
Borneo, 11, 23, 116, 187, 199, 200, 202, 205
Borneo, Bishop of, 95
Boyle, Frederick, 20
Brandes, Prof., 127, 143-4, 172, 179, 180, 183-6
Brooke, Sir James, 17, 20-3
Browne, Frank, 45
Bruen, D. L., 207
Brunei, 199
Buffon, Comte de, 12, 14

Camper, Petrus, 15-16

Celebes, 11
Chambers, 21
Chimpanzee *Viki*, 14
Collenette, Dr. P., 116
Copsychus malabaricus, 86
Cornwall, Nigel, 95
Crandall, Dr. Lee S., 181, 202

Daily Express, 173
Dawson, Charles, 12
Dayang, 37-8
Deli river, 142
Dubois, Eugène, 11

Emplanjau stream, 61
Ethiopia, 15

Fink, 160
Fisher, Dr. G. D., 131-2, 177
Fox, 183
Frederick II of Germany, 16

Gaun anak Sureng, 53-5, 88, 184
van Goens, 143-4, 146-7
Granada TV, 14
Greene, Prof. John C., 15
Gudgeon, L. W. W., 23

Hagenbeck, 160, 191-2
Haile, Dr. N. S., 207
Heck, Lutz, 192-3
Heck, H., 170
Hediger, Prof. Dr. Heini, 27, 51, 89, 125, 137, 168, 197
Hendrikson, Prof. John, 216
Heuvelmans, S., 13
Holliday, Mr. and Mrs., 148
Homo nocturnus, 15
  sylvestris orang-outang, 15
Hooijer, Dr. D. A., 11
Hornaday, William, 22

Ina, 36, 47, 54, 55
Indonesia, 205
Inger, Bob, 30
International Union of Directors of Zoological Gardens, 203

Jakeway, Derek, 129, 133
Java, 15, 203
Jones, Marvin, 214

Kadas, Barbara, 47
Kalimantun, 200
Keppel, Capt. Henry, 21
Kinabatangan river, 116, 200
Klös, Dr., 194
Koenigswald, Prof. Dr. G.H.R.V., 11
Krone Circus, 167
Kuching, 30, 35

Lambe, Admiral Sir Charles, 169
Letts, Charles, 140

Lingga river, 17, 21
Linnaeus, C., 14
Lundu, 37

Macaques, 59
Macpherson, Mrs., 132, 188
Maias, 17, 18, 58
  kesa, 61, 67-9
  rambai, 61, 68-9
  timbau, 61, 68-9
Malay Archipelago, 12
Marryat, Midshipman Frank, 21
Maugham, Somerset, 26
Max, 159
Medway, Lord, 11
Morris, Dr. Desmond, 169
Munday, Capt. Rodney, 20
Museum of Natural History in Paris, 16

Nature, 12
Niah, 11, 65, 114
Nimbun, 36
Nowell, Capt., 140, 155, 158

Oakley, Dr. Kenneth, 12
Orang-utan (Pongo pygmaeus), 8, 14
Orangs :
  Adam, 183
  Adriaan, 180, 182
  Bill, 45-6, 49, 91-2, 101-6, 110-13
  Blondy, 176
  Bob, 30, 33, 38-9, 40-1, 43, 46-8, 93, 174
  Bobby, 212
  Bonzo, 180, 182

Orangs [*contd.*]
  Buddha, 168
  Buschi, 179-80, 183-4
  Chief Utan, 176
  Cinderella, 176
  Cleo, 178-9, 183, 192
  Derek, 25, 133, 139, 148, 161, 188
  Eve, 25, 37-8, 41-4, 46, 48, 91-4,
    97, 193-5
  Frank, 45-6, 49, 91-3, 99, 101-
    14, 129-31, 133, 139, 191-2
  Goliath, 143, 183, 185
  Guarina, 176-7
  Guas, 176-7
  Hassan, 178
  Ivy, 176-7
  Jacob, 188
  Janie, 120, 122, 212
  Jenny, 194
  Jet, 182
  Jiggs, 171
  Jocky, 194
  Julchen, 181
  Julia, 180
  Lore, 167
  Lucky, 176
  Lucky II, 176
  Maggie, 176
  Martha, 202
  Mary, 177
  Mawas, 181
  Meja, 183-4
  Mickey, 131, 177
  Nigel, 25, 96-9, 100, 106, 110-
    14, 129-31, 139
  Noëll, 43-4, 48, 189
  Norsuto, 176
  Ossy, 25, 116, 120-5, 127-9, 133,
    139, 148-61, 187, 212

  Peter, 172
  Pinkie, 176-7
  Roberta, 212
  Rusty, 176-7
  Sandy, 172
  Suma, 180, 183-4
  Tineke, 180, 182
  Tony, 45
  Wambo, 181
Owen, Richard, 16

Palaeolithic, 11
Pendawan, 65, 87
Pig Lane, 32
Piltdown Man, 12
Plai (Bukit Plai), 55-6, 65
Pongo pygmaeus, 8, 14
Pournelle, Dr. George, 47
Prey, U., 168
Purchese, Cliff, 140, 142, 150-1,
  159
Pygathrix rubicundus, 58

Rejang river, 139
Rice, Mrs. Carol, 190
Ringling, John, 145, 187
Ruhe, H., 143-5
Ruhe, Louis, 186
Ryhiner, Peter, 203

Sabal Forest Reserve, 114
Sadong river, 61
Sarawak, 17, 201, 205, 207
Sarawak Museum, 11, 30, 201
Sarawak Museum Journal, 12, 88
Schaller, Dr. George, 201
Schneider, Gustav, 146, 147
Schomberg, Geoffrey, 163, 203

Sebangan, 85

Sebuyau, 55, 91

Seping, Stephen, 116

Shama, 86

Smythies, B. E., 45

Socotra, 139, 148

Spindler, Dr., 178

Street, Philip, 175, 189

Sumatra, 11, 143, 145-6, 187, 199

Summers, Lord John, 13

Sunday Times, 202

The Times, 25

Treecher, 21

Tribune, 95

Tring, 172

Tuba, 65, 87

Tulp, Nicholas, 12

Turtle Islands, 34

Tyson, Edward, 13-14

Ulmer, F. A., 172, 175

van Bemmel, Dr., 180, 182

van den Bergh, Dr., 113

van Goens, 143-4, 144, 146-7

Viki, 125

de Vries, Prof., 12

Wallace, Alfred Russel, 15-17, 19-20

Wenner Gren Foundation, 203

World Within, 25

Zedwitz, Graf, 178

Zoological Society of London, Transactions of, 16

Zoos :

Antwerp, 113

Berlin, 175, 178-9, 183, 192

Bronx, 25

Columbo, 203

Copenhagen, 202

Cros des Cagnes, 183, 185

Dresden, 121, 127-8, 143, 175, 181, 185

Düsseldorf, 124, 126, 175, 181, 183

Edinburgh, 131, 177, 187

Frankfurt, 116, 177, 179, 183

Hamburg, 131, 191

Havana, 175, 177

Hellabrunn, 169-70

Holland, 15

Johore, 111

London, 24, 159, 163, 166-7, 171, 188, 201

Manila, 111

Moscow, 175

New York, 181

Nürnberg, 122, 175

Philadelphia, 175, 183, 203-4

Pretoria, 25

Rome, 175

Rotterdam, 180, 182, 204

St. Louis, 175

San Diego, 43-4, 47, 113, 171, 174, 189, 204

Vienna, 178, 179

(See also Appendix IV)

Some other Oxford Paperbacks for readers interested in Central Asia, China, Japan, and South-East Asia, past and present

Cambodia

GEORGE COEDÈS
Angkor

MALCOLM MacDONALD
Angkor and the Khmers*

Central Asia

PETER FLEMING
Bayonets to Lhasa

ANDRÉ GUIBAUT
Tibetan Venture

LADY MACARTNEY
An English Lady in Chinese Turkestan

DIANA SHIPTON
The Antique Land

C. P. SKRINE AND
PAMELA NIGHTINGALE
Macartney at Kashgar*

ERIC TEICHMAN
Journey to Turkistan

ALBERT VON LE COQ
Buried Treasures of Chinese Turkestan

AITCHEN K. WU
Turkistan Tumult

China

All About Shanghai: A Standard Guide

L. C. ARLINGTON AND WILLIAM LEWISOHN
In Search of Old Peking

VICKI BAUM
Shanghai '37

ERNEST BRAMAH
Kai Lung's Golden Hours*

ERNEST BRAMAH
The Wallet of Kai Lung*

ANN BRIDGE
The Ginger Griffin

NIGEL CAMERON
The Chinese Smile

CHANG HSIN-HAI
The Fabulous Concubine*

CARL CROW
Handbook for China

PETER FLEMING
The Siege at Peking

ROBERT FORD
Captured in Tibet

MARY HOOKER
Behind the Scenes in Peking

NEALE HUNTER
Shanghai Journal*

GEORGE N. KATES
The Years that Were Fat

CORRINNE LAMB
The Chinese Festive Board

ALEKO LILIUS
I Sailed with Chinese Pirates

G. E. MORRISON
An Australian in China

DESMOND NEILL
Elegant Flower

PETER QUENNELL
A Superficial Journey through Tokyo and Peking

OSBERT SITWELL
Escape with Me! An Oriental Sketchbook

J. A. TURNER
Kwang Tung or Five Years in South China

JULES VERNE
The Tribulations of a Chinese Gentleman

Hong Kong and Macau

AUSTIN COATES
City of Broken Promises

AUSTIN COATES
A Macao Narrative

AUSTIN COATES
Macao and the British, 1637–1842

ÀUSTIN COATES
Myself a Mandarin

AUSTIN COATES
The Road

The Hong Kong Guide 1893

Indonesia

VICKI BAUM
A Tale from Bali*

'BENGAL CIVILIAN'
Rambles in Java and the Straits in 1852

VIOLET CLIFTON
Islands of Indonesia

MIGUEL COVARRUBIAS
Island of Bali*

AUGUSTA DE WIT
Java: Facts and Fancies

JACQUES DUMARÇAY
The Temples of Java

ANNA FORBES
Unbeaten Tracks in Islands of the Far East

HAROLD FORSTER
Flowering Lotus: A View of Java in the 1950s

GEOFFREY GORER
Bali and Angkor

JENNIFER LINDSAY
Javanese Gamelan

EDWIN M. LOEB
Sumatra: Its History and People

MOCHTAR LUBIS
Indonesia: Land under the Rainbow

MOCHTAR LUBIS
The Outlaw and Other Stories

MOCHTAR LUBIS
Twilight in Djakarta

MADELON H. LULOFS
Coolie

MADELON H. LULOFS
Rubber

COLIN McPHEE
A House in Bali*

H. W. PONDER
Java Pageant

H. W. PONDER
Javanese Panorama

JAN POORTENAAR
An Artist in Java and Other Islands of Indonesia

HICKMAN POWELL
The Last Paradise

F. M. SCHNITGER
Forgotten Kingdoms in Sumatra

E. R. SCIDMORE
Java, The Garden of the East

MICHAEL SMITHIES
Yogyakarta: Cultural Heart of Indonesia

LADISLAO SZÉKELY
Tropic Fever: The Adventures of a Planter in Sumatra

ALFRED RUSSEL WALLACE
The Malay Archipelago

HARRY WILCOX
Six Moons in Sulawesi

Japan

WILLIAM PLOMER
Sado

Malaysia

ODOARDO BECCARI
Wanderings in the Great Forests of Borneo

ISABELLA L. BIRD
The Golden Chersonese: Travels in Malaya in 1879

CARL BOCK
The Head-Hunters of Borneo

MARGARET BROOKE
THE RANEE OF SARAWAK
My Life in Sarawak

SYLVIA, LADY BROOKE
THE RANEE OF SARAWAK
Queen of the Head-hunters

F. W. BURBIDGE
The Gardens of the Sun

SIR HUGH CLIFFORD
Saleh: A Prince of Malaya

IVOR H. N. EVANS
Among Primitive Peoples in Borneo

HENRI FAUCONNIER
The Soul of Malaya

C. W. HARRISON
Illustrated Guide to the Federated Malay States (1923)

BARBARA HARRISSON
Orang-Utan

TOM HARRISSON
Borneo Jungle

TOM HARRISSON
World Within: A Borneo Story

CHARLES HOSE
Natural Man

W. SOMERSET MAUGHAM
Ah King and Other Stories*

W. SOMERSET MAUGHAM
The Casuarina Tree*

ROBERT PAYNE
The White Rajahs of Sarawak

Philippines

LEON WOLFF
Little Brown Brother

Singapore

RUSSELL GRENFELL
Main Fleet to Singapore

MASANOBU TSUJI
Singapore 1941–1942

C. W. WURTZBURG
Raffles of the Eastern Isles

Thailand

CARL BOCK
Temples and Elephants

ANNA LEONOWENS
The English Governess at the Siamese Court

SIBURAPHA
Behind the Painting and Other Stories

MALCOLM SMITH
A Physician at the Court of Siam

ERNEST YOUNG
The Kingdom of the Yellow Robe

* Titles marked with an asterisk have restricted rights.